JUMP Math 4.2

Book 4 Part 2 of 2

Contents

Patterns and Algebra 2 175

Number Sense 2 200

Measurement 2 286

Probability and Data Management 2 304

Geometry 2 321

jump math™

MULTIPLYING POTENTIAL.

Contents

PART 1
Patterns & Algebra

PA4-1	Counting	1
PA4-2	Preparation for Increasing Sequences	3
PA4-3	Increasing Sequences	4
PA4-4	Counting Backwards	5
PA4-5	Decreasing Sequences	7
PA4-6	Increasing and Decreasing Sequences	8
PA4-7	Attributes	9
PA4-8	Repeating Patterns	11
PA4-9	Extending a Pattern Using a Rule	12
PA4-10	Identifying Pattern Rules	13
PA4-11	Introduction to T-tables	14
PA4-12	T-tables	16
PA4-13	Patterns Involving Time	19
PA4-14	Problem Solving with Patterns	21

Number Sense

NS4-1	Place Value – Ones, Tens, Hundreds and Thousands	22
NS4-2	Place Value	23
NS4-3	Writing Numbers	24
NS4-4	Representation with Base Ten Materials	26
NS4-5	Representation in Expanded Form	28
NS4-6	Representing Numbers (Review)	31
NS4-7	Comparing Numbers	32
NS4-8	Comparing and Ordering Numbers	33
NS4-9	Differences of 10, 100, and 1 000	35
NS4-10	Differences of 10, 100, and 1 000 (Advanced)	36
NS4-11	Counting by 10s, 100s and 1 000s	37
NS4-12	Comparing Numbers (Advanced)	38
NS4-13	Regrouping	39
NS4-14	Adding 2-Digit Numbers	42
NS4-15	Adding with Regrouping (or Carrying)	43
NS4-16	Adding with Money	45
NS4-17	Adding 3-Digit Numbers	46
NS4-18	Adding 4-Digit Numbers	48
NS4-19	Subtraction	50
NS4-20	Subtracting by Regrouping	52
NS4-21	Parts and Totals	56
NS4-22	Parts and Totals (Advanced)	57

NS4-23	Sums and Differences	58
NS4-24	Larger Numbers (Advanced)	59
NS4-25	Concepts in Number Sense	60
NS4-26	Arrays	61
NS4-27	Multiplication and Addition	62
NS4-28	Multiplying by Skip Counting & Adding On	64
NS4-29	Multiplying by Adding On	65
NS4-30	Multiples of 10	67
NS4-31	Advanced Arrays	68
NS4-32	Mental Math	69
NS4-33	Mental Math: Doubling	70
NS4-34	The Standard Method for Multiplication	71
NS4-35	Regrouping (Multiplication)	72
NS4-36	Multiplying a 3-Digit by a 1-Digit Number	73
NS4-37	Topics in Multiplication	74
NS4-38	Concepts in Multiplication	75
NS4-39	Rounding on a Number Line	76
NS4-40	Rounding on a Number Line (Hundreds)	78
NS4-41	Rounding on a Number Line (Thousands)	79
NS4-42	Rounding	80
NS4-43	Rounding on a Grid	82
NS4-44	Estimating Sums and Differences	83
NS4-45	Estimating	84
NS4-46	More Estimating	85
NS4-47	Counting Coins	86
NS4-48	Counting by Different Denominations	89
NS4-49	Least Number of Coins	91
NS4-50	Making Change Using Mental Math	93
NS4-51	Organized Lists	95

Measurement

ME4-1	Estimating Lengths in Centimetres	97
ME4-2	Measuring in Centimetres	98
ME4-3	Drawing and Measuring in Centimetres	99
ME4-4	Estimating in Millimetres	100
ME4-5	Millimetres and Centimetres	101
ME4-6	Comparing Centimetres and Millimetres	103
ME4-7	Centimetres and Millimetres (Advanced)	104
ME4-8	Problems and Puzzles	105
ME4-9	Metres	106
ME4-10	Metres (Advanced)	107
ME4-11	Kilometres	108
ME4-12	Kilometres and Metres	109

ME4-13	Ordering and Assigning Appropriate Units	110
ME4-14	Ordering Units – Metres and Centimetres	111
ME4-15	More Ordering & Assigning Appropriate Units	112
ME4-16	Perimeter	114
ME4-17	Exploring Perimeter	116
ME4-18	Measuring Perimeter	117
ME4-19	Telling Time (Review)	119
ME4-20	Telling Time (Half and Quarter Hours)	121
ME4-21	Telling Time in Two Ways	122
ME4-22	Telling Time (One-Minute Intervals)	123
ME4-23	Elapsed Time	125
ME4-24	Elapsed Time (Advanced)	126
ME4-25	Times of Day	127
ME4-26	The 24-Hour Clock	128
ME4-27	Time Intervals	129
ME4-28	Longer Time Intervals	130
ME4-29	Topics in Time	131

Probability & Data Management

PDM4-1	Introduction to Classifying Data	132
PDM4-2	Venn Diagrams	133
PDM4-3	Venn Diagrams (Advanced)	135
PDM4-4	Revisiting Pictographs	136
PDM4-5	Choosing a Pictograph Scale and Symbol	138
PDM4-6	Pictographs (Advanced)	139
PDM4-7	Introduction to Bar Graphs	140
PDM4-8	Choosing a Scale for a Bar Graph	142
PDM4-9	Double Bar Graphs	143
PDM4-10	Surveys	144
PDM4-11	Designing Your Own Survey	145
PDM4-12	Reading and Manipulating Found Data	147

Geometry

G4-1	Sides and Vertices of 2-D Figures	148
G4-2	Introduction to Angles	150
G4-3	Special Angles	152
G4-4	Measuring Angles	153
G4-5	Parallel Lines	156
G4-6	Quadrilaterals	158
G4-7	Properties of Shapes	159
G4-8	Special Quadrilaterals	161
G4-9	Tangrams	163

G4-10	Congruency	164
G4-11	Congruency (Advanced)	165
G4-12	Symmetry	166
G4-13	Symmetry and Paper Folding	167
G4-14	More Symmetry	168
G4-15	Triangles	169
G4-16	Comparing Shapes	170
G4-17	Sorting and Classifying Shapes	171
G4-18	Sorting and Classifying Shapes (Review)	173
G4-19	Puzzles and Problems	174

PART 2
Patterns & Algebra

PA4-15	Number Lines	175
PA4-16	Number Lines (Advanced)	176
PA4-17	Extending and Predicting Positions	177
PA4-18	Describing and Creating Patterns	180
PA4-19	Describing and Creating Patterns (Advanced)	181
PA4-20	2-Dimensional Patterns	183
PA4-21	2-Dimensional Patterns (Advanced)	185
PA4-22	Calendars	187
PA4-23	Patterns in the Two Times Tables	188
PA4-24	Patterns in the Five Times Tables	189
PA4-25	Patterns in the Eight Times Tables	190
PA4-26	Patterns in the Times Tables (Advanced)	191
PA4-27	Patterns with Increasing and Decreasing Steps	192
PA4-28	Advanced Patterns	193
PA4-29	Patterns with Larger Numbers	194
PA4-30	Introduction to Algebra	195
PA4-31	Algebra	196
PA4-32	Algebra (Advanced)	197
PA4-33	Problems and Puzzles	198

Number Sense

NS4-52	Sets	200
NS4-53	Sharing – Knowing the Number of Sets	202
NS4-54	Sharing – Knowing the Number in Each Set	203
NS4-55	Two Ways of Sharing	204
NS4-56	Division and Addition	207
NS4-57	Dividing by Skip Counting	208
NS4-58	The Two Meanings of Division	209
NS4-59	Division and Multiplication	211

NS4-60	Knowing When to Multiply or Divide (Introduction)	212
NS4-61	Knowing When to Multiply or Divide	213
NS4-62	Remainders	215
NS4-63	Finding Remainders on Number Lines	217
NS4-64	Mental Math – Division	218
NS4-65	Long Division – 2-Digit by 1-Digit	219
NS4-66	Further Division	224
NS4-67	Unit Rates	225
NS4-68	Concepts in Multiplication and Division	226
NS4-69	Systematic Search	227
NS4-70	Naming of Fractions	228
NS4-71	Equal Parts and Models of Fractions	229
NS4-72	Equal Parts of a Set	230
NS4-73	Parts and Wholes	232
NS4-74	Ordering and Comparing Fractions	233
NS4-75	More Ordering and Comparing Fractions	234
NS4-76	Parts and Wholes (Advanced)	235
NS4-77	Mixed Fractions	236
NS4-78	Improper Fractions	237
NS4-79	Mixed and Improper Fractions	238
NS4-80	Investigating Mixed & Improper Fractions	239
NS4-81	Mixed Fractions (Advanced)	241
NS4-82	Mixed and Improper Fractions (Advanced)	242
NS4-83	Equivalent Fractions	243
NS4-84	More Equivalent Fractions	244
NS4-85	Further Equivalent Fractions	245
NS4-86	Sharing and Fractions	246
NS4-87	More Sharing and Fractions	248
NS4-88	Sharing and Fractions (Advanced)	249
NS4-89	More Mixed and Improper Fractions	250
NS4-90	Adding and Subtracting Fractions (Introduction)	251
NS4-91	Fractions Review	252
NS4-92	Dollar and Cent Notation	253
NS4-93	Converting Between Dollar and Cent Notation	255
NS4-94	More Dollar and Cent Notation	256
NS4-95	Canadian Bills and Coins	257
NS4-96	Adding Money	258
NS4-97	Subtracting Money	260
NS4-98	Estimating	261
NS4-99	Decimal Tenths	263
NS4-100	Place Values (Decimals)	264
NS4-101	Decimal Hundredths	265
NS4-102	Tenths and Hundredths	266

NS4-103	Changing Tenths to Hundredths	267
NS4-104	Decimals and Money	268
NS4-105	Changing Notation: Fractions and Decimals	269
NS4-106	Decimals and Fractions Greater Than One	270
NS4-107	Decimals and Fractions on Number Lines	271
NS4-108	Comparing Fractions and Decimals	272
NS4-109	Ordering Fractions and Decimals	273
NS4-110	Adding and Subtracting Tenths	275
NS4-111	Adding Hundredths	276
NS4-112	Subtracting Hundredths	277
NS4-113	Adding and Subtracting Decimals (Review)	278
NS4-114	Differences of 0.1 and 0.01	279
NS4-115	Order and Place Value (Advanced)	280
NS4-116	Concepts in Decimals	281
NS4-117	Dividing by 10 and 100	282
NS4-118	Changing Units	283
NS4-119	Exploring Numbers	284
NS4-120	Word Problems	285

Measurement

ME4-30	Area in Square Centimetres	286
ME4-31	Area of Rectangles	287
ME4-32	Exploring Area	288
ME4-33	Area with Half Squares	289
ME4-34	Finding and Estimating Area	290
ME4-35	Comparing Area and Perimeter	291
ME4-36	Area and Perimeter	292
ME4-37	Problems and Puzzles	293
ME4-38	Volume	294
ME4-39	Volume of Rectangular Prisms	295
ME4-40	Mass	297
ME4-41	Changing Units of Mass	299
ME4-42	Problems Involving Mass	300
ME4-43	Capacity	301
ME4-44	Mass and Capacity	302
ME4-45	Temperature	303

Probability & Data Management

PDM4-13	Range and Median	304
PDM4-14	The Mean	305
PDM4-15	Stem and Leaf Plots	307
PDM4-16	Outcomes	310

PDM4-17	Even Chances	311
PDM4-18	Even, Likely and Unlikely	313
PDM4-19	Equal Likelihood	314
PDM4-20	Describing Probability	315
PDM4-21	Fair Games	317
PDM4-22	Expectation	318
PDM4-23	Problems and Puzzles	320

Geometry

G4-20	Introduction to Coordinate Systems	321
G4-21	Introduction to Slides	323
G4-22	Slides	324
G4-23	Slides (Advanced)	325
G4-24	Grids and Maps	326
G4-25	Games and Activities with Maps and Grids	329
G4-26	Reflections	330
G4-27	Reflections (Advanced)	331
G4-28	Rotations	332
G4-29	Rotations (Advanced)	333
G4-30	Building Pyramids	334
G4-31	Building Prisms	335
G4-32	Edges, Vertices, and Faces	336
G4-33	Prisms and Pyramids	338
G4-34	Prism and Pyramid Bases	339
G4-35	Properties of Pyramids and Prisms	341
G4-36	Nets	344
G4-37	Sorting 3-D Shapes	345
G4-38	Isoparametric Drawings	346
G4-39	Isometric Drawings	347
G4-40	Geometry in the World	348
G4-41	Problems and Puzzles	349

Children will need to answer the questions marked with a ▢ in a notebook. Grid paper and notebooks should always be on hand for answering extra questions or when additional room for calculation is needed. Grid paper is also available in the BLM section of the Teacher's Guide.

The ⬡ means "Stop! Assess understanding and explain new concepts before proceeding."

PA4-15: Number Lines

Marie is on a bicycle tour 300 km from home. She can cycle 75 km each day.

She starts riding towards home on Tuesday morning.
How far away from home will she be by Thursday evening?

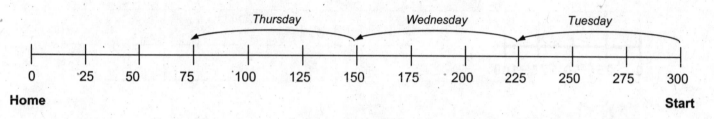

On Thursday evening, Marie will be 75 km from home.

- -

1. On Wednesday morning Ryan's campsite is 20 km from Mount Currie in BC.

   He plans to walk 6 km towards the mountain each day.

   How far from the mountain will he be on Thursday evening? _____

   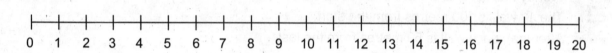

2. Jane is camping 50 km from her home.
   She can cycle 15 km every hour.
   How far from home will she be after 3 hours? _____

   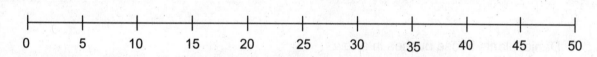

Draw and label a number line in the grid to solve the following problems.

3. Midori is 16 blocks from home. She can bike 4 blocks in a minute.

   How far from home will she be after 3 minutes? _____

4. Tom lives 12 blocks from the park. He can rollerblade 2 blocks per minute.

   How many minutes will it take him to rollerblade to the park? _____

   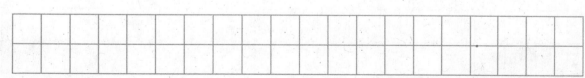

PA4-16: Number Lines (Advanced)

In the questions below, you will have to decide on a scale for your number lines.

1. James has entered a 250 km bicycle race. He can cycle 75 km each day.
   How far from the finish will he be after 3 days? _____

   0   25   50   75   100

2. Sudha is typing an essay. It is 250 words long. She can type 25 words per minute.
   How long does she take to type the whole assignment? _____

3. Wendy has to climb 5 walls in an obstacle course.
   The 1st wall is 100 metres from the start.
   After that, each wall is 50 metres from the last.
   How far from the start is the 3rd wall? _____

4. Daniel plants 5 rose bushes in a row.
   The nearest bush is 10 metres from his house. The bushes are 5 m apart.
   How far away from Daniel's house is the last bush? _____
   HINT: Put Daniel's house at zero on the number line.

5. A painter's ladder has 12 steps.
   The painter spills red paint on every second step and blue paint on every third step.
   Which steps have red and blue paint on them? _____

Patterns & Algebra 2

1. Karen makes a repeating pattern using red (**R**) and yellow (**Y**) blocks.
   The box shows the core of her pattern.
   Continue the pattern by writing Rs and Ys.

a)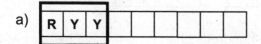

b)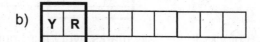

c)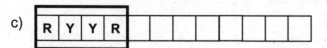

d)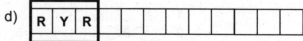

e)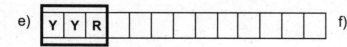

f)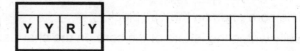

2. Stan tried to continue the pattern in the box. Did he continue the pattern correctly?
   HINT: Shade the reds (R) if it helps.

a)

YES NO

b)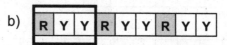

YES NO

c)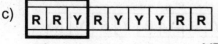

YES NO

d)

YES NO

e)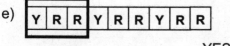

YES NO

f)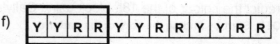

YES NO

3. For each pattern below, say whether the blocks in the rectangle are the <u>core</u> of the pattern.

a)

YES NO

b)

YES NO

c)

YES NO

d)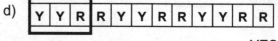

YES NO

e)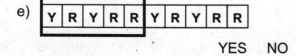

YES NO

f)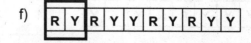

YES NO

PA4-17: Extending and Predicting Positions (continued)

Sally wants to predict the colour of the 17th block in the pattern. First she finds the core of the pattern.

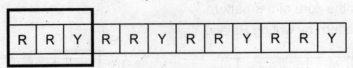

The core is 3 blocks long. Sally marks every <u>third</u> number on a hundreds chart.

Each X shows the position of
a block where the core ends:

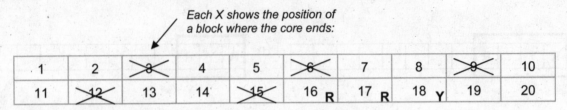

The core ends on the 15th block.

Sally writes the letters of the core on the chart, starting at 16.

The 17th block is red.

- -

4. In the patterns below, put a rectangle around the blocks that make up the core.

a) | Y | R | R | Y | R | R | Y | R | R |

b) | R | R | R | Y | R | R | R | Y | R |

c) | Y | Y | R | R | Y | Y | R | R | Y | Y | R | R |

d) | Y | R | R | Y | Y | R | R | Y |

e) | R | Y | R | Y | Y | Y | R | Y | R | Y | Y | Y |

f) | R | Y | R | Y | R | Y | R | Y | R |

5. Predict the colour of the 18th block using Sally's method.
   NOTE: Start by finding the core of the pattern.

| R | Y | Y | Y | R | Y | Y | Y |

Colour: _____

1	2	3	4	5	6	7	8	9	10
11	12	13	14	15	16	17	18	19	20

6. Predict the colour of the 19th block.

| R | R | Y | Y | R | R | Y | Y |

Colour: _____

1	2	3	4	5	6	7	8	9	10
11	12	13	14	15	16	17	18	19	20

7. Predict the colour of the 17th block.

| R | R | Y | Y | Y | R | R | Y | Y | Y |

Colour: _____

1	2	3	4	5	6	7	8	9	10
11	12	13	14	15	16	17	18	19	20

8. Draw a box around the <u>core</u> of the pattern. Then predict the colour of the 35th block.

| Y | R | Y | Y | R | Y | Y | R | Y |

Colour: _____

1	2	3	4	5	6	7	8	9	10
11	12	13	14	15	16	17	18	19	20
21	22	23	24	25	26	27	28	29	30
31	32	33	34	35	36	37	38	39	40

TEACHER:
Your students will need a copy of the hundreds charts page from the Teacher's Guide.

9. Carl makes a pattern with red, white, and blue beads.

What colour will the 41st bead be?

10. Angie makes a pattern with triangles.

Will the 22nd triangle in her pattern point up or down? How do you know?

11. What is the 31st coin in this pattern?

12. a) What is the 15th coin in this pattern? Explain how you know.

BONUS
b) What is the total value of the first 15 coins?
    HINT: Try grouping coins together rather than adding one coin at a time.

PA4-18: Describing and Creating Patterns

In this sequence, each number is greater than the one before it: **7 , 8 , 10 , 15 , 21**
The sequence is always **increasing**.

In this sequence, each number is less than the one before it: **25 , 23 , 18 , 11 , 8**
The sequence is always **decreasing**.

----

1. Write a **+** sign in the circle to show where the sequence <u>increases</u>.
    Write a **−** sign to show where it <u>decreases</u>.

    a) 6 (+) , 9 (−) , 7 (+) , 11   b) 1 ○ , 5 ○ , 7 ○ , 2   c) 10 ○ , 7 ○ , 6 ○ , 8

    d) 2 ○ , 5 ○ , 1 ○ , 7   e) 5 ○ , 3 ○ , 9 ○ , 8   f) 2 ○ , 5 ○ , 9 ○ , 12

    g) 2 ○ , 7 ○ , 4 ○ , 9   h) 11 ○ , 15 ○ , 18 ○ , 13   i) 18 ○ , 13 ○ , 11 ○ , 23

    j) 28 ○ , 36 ○ , 49 ○ , 52   k) 17 ○ , 38 ○ , 29 ○ , 85   l) 53 ○ , 64 ○ , 96 ○ , 98

2. Write a **+** sign in the circle to show where the sequence <u>increases</u>.
    Write a **−** sign to show where it <u>decreases</u>. Then write ...

    ... an **A** beside the sequence if it <u>increases</u>

    ... a **B** beside the sequence if it <u>decreases</u>

    ... a **C** beside the sequence if it <u>increases</u> and <u>decreases</u>.

    a) 4 (+) , 8 (−) , 3 (+) , 7   _C_

    2 ○ , 8 ○ , 9 ○ 11   _____

    10 ○ , 9 ○ , 4 ○ 1   _____

    b) 7 ○ , 5 ○ , 3 ○ , 2   _____

    8 ○ , 6 ○ , 3 ○ , 9   _____

    1 ○ , 4 ○ , 7 ○ 11   _____

    c) 3 ○ , 4 ○ , 6 ○ , 8   _____

    8 ○ , 4 ○ , 2 ○ , 7   _____

    9 ○ , 5 ○ , 1 ○ , 0   _____

    d) 17 ○ , 14 ○ , 12 ○ , 10   _____

    20 ○ , 24 ○ , 15 ○ , 29   _____

    23 ○ , 29 ○ , 34 ○ 40   _____

Patterns & Algebra 2

1. Find the <u>amount</u> by which the sequence <u>increases</u> or <u>decreases</u>.
   (Write a number with a **+** sign if the sequence increases, and a **–** sign if it decreases.)

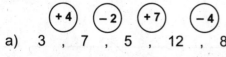

a) 3 , 7 , 5 , 12 , 8

b) 2 , 5 , 4 , 8 , 5

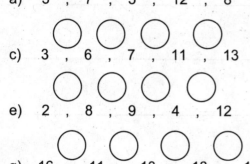

c) 3 , 6 , 7 , 11 , 13

e) 2 , 8 , 9 , 4 , 12

g) 16 , 11 , 13 , 18 , 15

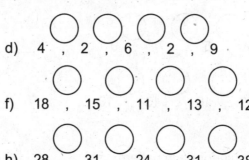

d) 4 , 2 , 6 , 2 , 9

f) 18 , 15 , 11 , 13 , 12

h) 28 , 31 , 24 , 31 , 38

2. Match each sequence with the sentence that describes it. This sequence ...

a) A   ... increases by 3 each time.
    B   ... increases by different amounts.

    ____   9 , 12 , 15 , 18 , 21

    ____   7 , 10 , 13 , 14 , 19

b) A   ... increases by 4 each time.
    B   ... increases by different amounts.

    ____   6 , 10 , 14 , 17 , 21

    ____   5 , 9 , 13 , 17 , 21

c) A   ... decreases by 5 each time.
    B   ... decreases by different amounts.

    ____   35 , 30 , 25 , 20 , 15

    ____   30 , 25 , 20 , 15 , 5

d) A   ... decreases by different amounts.
    B   ... decreases by the same amount.

    ____   10 , 9 , 8 , 6 , 5

    ____   11 , 10 , 9 , 8 , 7

BONUS

e) A   ... increases by 5 each time.
    B   ... decreases by different amounts.
    C   ... increases by different amounts.

    ____   17 , 22 , 28 , 32 , 34

    ____   17 , 14 , 10 , 9 , 6

    ____   14 , 19 , 24 , 29 , 34

f) A   ... increases and decreases.
    B   ... increases by the same amount.
    C   ... decreases by different amounts.
    D   ... decreases by the same amount.

    ____   21 , 19 , 15 , 13 , 9

    ____   10 , 13 , 9 , 7 , 5

    ____   19 , 17 , 15 , 13 , 11

    ____   9 , 12 , 15 , 18 , 21

3. Write a rule for each pattern. Use the words <u>add</u> or <u>subtract</u>, and be sure to say what number the pattern starts with.

a) 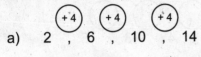 2 , 6 , 10 , 14   <u>Start at 2, add 4</u>

b) 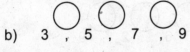 3 , 5 , 7 , 9   _____

c) 19 , 16 , 13 , 10   _____

4. Write a rule for each pattern.
   NOTE: One sequence doesn't have a rule – see if you can find it.

a) 8 , 11 , 14 , 17   _____

b) 14 , 10 , 6 , 2   _____

c) 25 , 21 , 18 , 17 , 11   _____

d) 61 , 65 , 69 , 73   _____

5. Describe each pattern as <u>increasing</u>, <u>decreasing</u> or <u>repeating</u>.

a) 1 , 4 , 7 , 10 , 13 , 16   b) 1 , 5 , 8 , 1 , 5 , 8

c) 9 , 8 , 7 , 6 , 5 , 4   d) 2 , 4 , 6 , 8 , 10 , 12

e) 3 , 8 , 3 , 8 , 3 , 8   f) 21 , 16 , 10 , 7 , 5 , 1

6. Write the first five numbers in each of the patterns described.
   a) Start at 6, add 3   b) Start at 26, subtract 4   c) Start at 39, add 5

7. Create an increasing or a decreasing number pattern. Give the rule for your pattern.

8. Create a repeating pattern using…   a) letters   b) shapes   c) numbers

9. Create a pattern and ask a friend to find the rule for your pattern.

1.

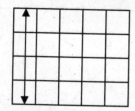

Columns run up and down.

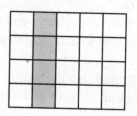

1st 2nd 3rd 4th 5th

Columns are numbered left to right (in this exercise).

The 2nd column is shaded.

Shade ...

a)

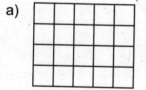

the 1st column.

b)

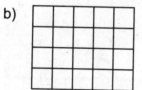

the 5th column.

c)

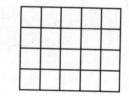

the 3rd column.

d)

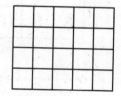

the 4th column.

2.

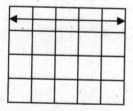

Rows run sideways.

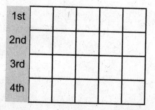

1st
2nd
3rd
4th

Rows are numbered from top to bottom (in this exercise).

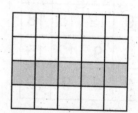

The 3rd row is shaded.

Shade ...

a)

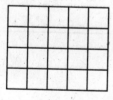

the 2nd row.

b)

the 4th row.

c)

the 1st row.

d)

the 3rd row.

3. Shade ...

a)

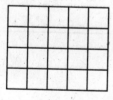

2	4	6
8	10	12
14	16	18

the 2nd row.

b)

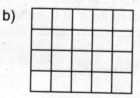

2	4	6
8	10	12
14	16	18

the 1st column.

c)

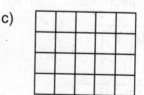

2	4	6
8	10	12
14	16	18

the 3rd column.

d)

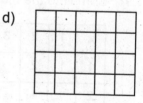

2	4	6
8	10	12
14	16	18

the diagonals
(one is shaded).

4. Describe the pattern in the numbers you shaded for each part of Question 3.

Patterns & Algebra 2

Describe the patterns you see in each chart below
(remember to look horizontally, vertically and diagonally).

You should use the words "rows," "columns," and
"diagonals" in your answers.

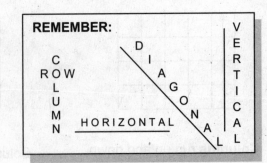

REMEMBER:

5.

2	4	6
4	6	8
6	8	10

6.

12	15	18	21
9	12	15	18
6	9	12	15
3	6	9	12

7. Complete the multiplication chart.

×	1	2	3	4	5	6
1	1	2				
2		4				
3		6				
4						
5						
6						

a) Describe the patterns you see in the rows, columns, and diagonals of the chart:

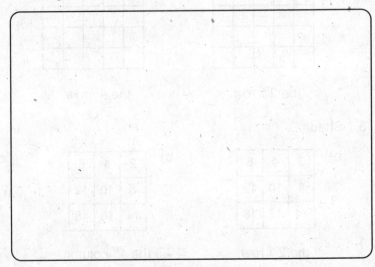

b) Each number in the third row of the chart is the sum of the numbers in the two rows above it.
Can you find any other relations between the rows or columns in the chart?

1. Place the letters A, B, and C so that each row and each column has exactly one A, one B, and one C in it (in any order).

2. Place the letters A and B so that each row and each column has two As and two Bs in it.

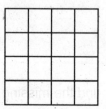

3.

Row 1	L	R	T	T	L
Row 2	R	T	T		
Row 3					
Row 4					
Row 5					
Row 6					
Row 7					

A gardener plants roses (R), lilies (L), and tulips (T) in rows in the pattern shown to the left.

a) Complete the chart.

b) In which row will the pattern in the second row be repeated?

_____

4. a) Shade every third square on a hundreds chart. **(These are the multiples of 3.)**
    How can you describe the position of the squares you shaded?

    b) Mark every fifth square on the same chart with an 'X'. **(These are the multiples of 5.)**

    c) Write out the numbers between 1 and 100 that are **multiples** of 3 and 5.
    Describe the pattern in the tens digit and in the ones digits of the numbers.

5. The "multiples of 3" are also called the numbers that are "divisible by 3."
    Complete the chart below by inserting the whole numbers from 1 to 20 into the correct boxes.

	Less than 11	Greater than or equal to 11
Divisible by 3		
Not divisible by 3		

PA4-21: 2-Dimensional Patterns (Advanced) *(continued)*

6. Here are some number pyramids:

   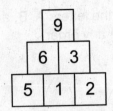

Can you find the rule by which the patterns in the pyramids were made? Describe it here.

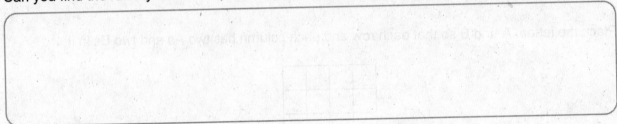

7. Using the rule you described in Question 6, find the missing numbers.

a)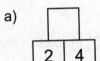

b)

c)

d)

e)

f)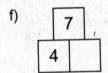

g)

h)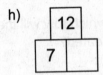

i)

j)

k)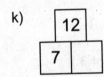

l)

m)

n)

o)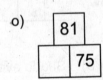

BONUS

p)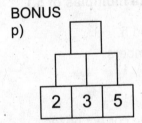

q)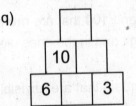

r)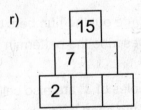

s)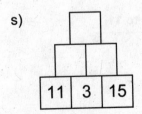

t)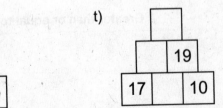

u)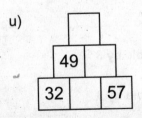

jump math
MULTIPLYING POTENTIAL

PA4-22: Calendars

TEACHER:
Your students will each need two copies of the Calendar blackline master from the Teacher's Guide.

<u>Months with 31 days</u>: **January, March, May, July, August, October, December.**

<u>Months with 30 days</u>: **April, June, September, November.**

<u>Months with 28 days</u>: **February (during a leap year, February has 29 days).**

- -

1. a) Write the title "December" on a blank calendar. Write the numbers of the days so that December 1st is a Wednesday.

   b) Rona has guitar lessons every <u>fourth</u> day of the month starting on December 4th. Mark the days when she has a guitar lesson with an 'X.'

2. April 1st is a Sunday.

   Huyan receives an allowance of $5 every Tuesday.

   How much money has he received by the end of the month? _____

3. The first day of October is a Tuesday.

   Alex has piano lessons every 6th day of the month starting on October 6th.

   Dan has lessons every Friday.

   On which dates do they have lessons on the same day? _____

4. Fill in the calendar for any month you choose. Shade the numbers along any column of the calendar.

Name of Month: _____

Sunday	Monday	Tuesday	Wednesday	Thursday	Friday	Saturday

   a) What pattern do you see? Write a rule for the pattern.

   _____

   b) Look at any other column. How do you explain what you see?

   _____

Patterns & Algebra 2

PA4-23: Patterns in the Two Times Tables

1. On a hundreds chart, shade the **multiples** of 2 (the numbers you say when counting by 2s: 2, 4, ...).

2. What patterns can you see in the <u>positions</u> of the multiples of two?
   Use the words *rows*, *columns*, or *diagonals* in your answer.

3. Look at the <u>ones digits</u> of the multiples of two in the third row of the hundreds chart.

21	**22**	23	2**4**	25	2**6**	27	2**8**	29	3**0**

   Underline the ones digits of the multiples of two in any other row. What do you notice?

4. How can you tell whether a number between 1 and 100 is a multiple of two without counting up?

5. The multiples of two (including zero) are called **even** numbers. Circle the even numbers.

   7   3   18   32   21   76   30   89   94   67   15   82

6. The numbers that are <u>not</u> multiples of two are called **odd** numbers. Circle the odd numbers.

   5   75   60   37   44   68   83   92   100

7. Pick an <u>even</u> number. Add two to your number. What kind of number do you get? Even or odd?
   Will this always happen?

Patterns & Algebra 2

PA4-24: Patterns in the Five Times Tables

1. On a hundreds chart, shade the **multiples** of 5 (the numbers you say when counting by 5s).

2. What patterns can you see in the <u>positions</u> of the multiples of five?
   Use the words *rows*, *columns*, or *diagonals* in your answer.

3. Look at the <u>ones digits</u> of the multiples of five in the fourth row of the hundreds chart.

31	32	33	34	3**5**	36	37	38	39	4**0**

   Now look at the ones digits of the multiples of five in any other row. What do you notice?

4. How can you tell whether a number between 1 and 100 is a multiple of five without counting up?

5. Circle the numbers that are multiples of five.

   8   16   45   27   60   62   90   85   11   25   50   37

6. Are all multiples of 5 even? Explain.

7. Circle the multiples of 5.

   203   205   217   225   385   426   589   755   931

PA4-25: Patterns in the Eight Times Tables

1. On a hundreds chart, shade the **multiples** of 8 (the numbers you say when counting by 8s).

2. Complete the following:

Write the **first five** multiples of eight here (in increasing order).
$\left\{\begin{array}{cc} \underline{0}\ \ \underline{8} \\ \underline{1}\ \ \underline{6} \\ \underline{\ \ }\ \ \underline{\ \ } \\ \underline{\ \ }\ \ \underline{\ \ } \\ \underline{\ \ }\ \ \underline{\ \ } \\ \uparrow \end{array}\right.$
$\left.\begin{array}{cc} \underline{\ \ }\ \ \underline{\ \ } \\ \underline{\ \ }\ \ \underline{\ \ } \\ \underline{\ \ }\ \ \underline{\ \ } \\ \underline{\ \ }\ \ \underline{\ \ } \\ \underline{\ \ }\ \ \underline{\ \ } \\ \uparrow \end{array}\right\}$
Write the **next five** multiples of eight here.

Look down the columns marked by the arrows. What pattern do you see in the <u>ones</u> digits?

3. What pattern do you see in the number of tens?

TEACHER:
Review the answers to Questions 2 and 3 above before allowing your students to go further.

4. Use the pattern you found in Questions 2 and 3 to write out the multiples of 8 from 88 to 160.

_ _   _ _ _

_ _   _ _ _

_ _ _   _ _ _

_ _ _   _ _ _

_ _ _   _ _ _

jump math
MULTIPLYING POTENTIAL.

Patterns & Algebra 2

PA4-26: Patterns in the Times Tables (Advanced)

TEACHER:
Review Venn diagrams with your students before assigning the question below.

1. a) Sort the numbers below into the Venn diagram. (The first number has been done for you.)

10	25	15	37	86	49	5	79	24
50	6	17	61	40	36	65	8	96

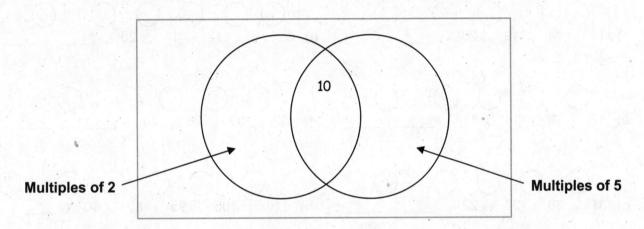

Multiples of 2   10   Multiples of 5

b) Think of two numbers from 50 to 100 that would go in the middle of the diagram: _____ , _____

c) Think of two numbers from 50 to 100 that could not be placed in either circle: _____ , _____

2. Sort the numbers below into the Venn diagram.

32	40	57	24	25	80	62	17	16
56	60	35	48	8	75	72	30	5

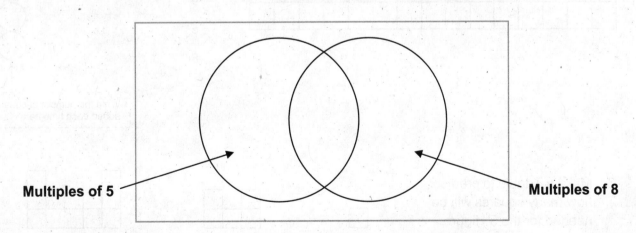

Multiples of 5   Multiples of 8

Patterns & Algebra 2

1. In the sequences below, the step or gap between the numbers increases or decreases.
   Can you see a pattern in the way the gap changes?
   Use the pattern to extend the sequence.

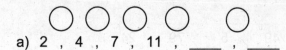

a) 2 , 4 , 7 , 11 , ___ , ___

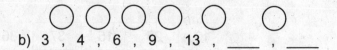

b) 3 , 4 , 6 , 9 , 13 , ___ , ___

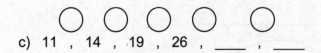

c) 11 , 14 , 19 , 26 , ___ , ___

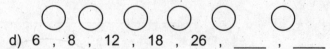

d) 6 , 8 , 12 , 18 , 26 , ___ , ___

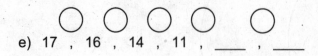

e) 17 , 16 , 14 , 11 , ___ , ___

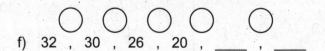

f) 32 , 30 , 26 , 20 , ___ , ___

g) 31 , 30 , 27 , 22 , ___ , ___

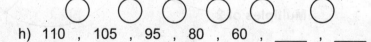

h) 110 , 105 , 95 , 80 , 60 , ___ , ___

2. Complete the T-table for the 3rd and 4th figures.
   Then use the pattern in the gap to predict the number of shaded squares in the 5th and 6th figures.

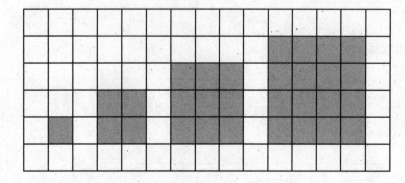

Figure	Number of Squares
1	1
2	4
3	
4	
5	
6	

Write the number of squares added each time here

3. Make a T-table to predict
   how many squares will be
   needed for the 5th figure.

  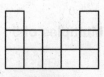

Figure 1   Figure 2   Figure 3

1. Ahmed made a pattern starting at 2.

    2 , 4 , 8 , 16 , ____ , ____ , ____ , ____

    a) What number did Ahmed multiply each term by to get the next term? _____

    b) Continue Ahmed's pattern.

    c) Find the gap between the numbers. What do you notice? _____

2. Olivia and Krishna save the amounts shown in the chart below.

Week	Olivia	Krishna
1	$1	$15
2	$2	$20
3	$4	$25
4	$8	$30
5		
6		
7		

    a) What is the pattern rule for the amount Krishna saves?

    _____

    b) What is the pattern rule for the amount Olivia saves?

    _____

    c) Who do you think will save more by the end of the seven weeks?

    _____

    d) Continue the patterns in the chart. Were you right?

    _____

3. 3 , 6 , 4 , 7 , 5 , 8 , ____ , ____ , ____

    a) Describe how the gap changes in the pattern above. _____

    _____

    b) Fill in the blanks to continue the pattern.

4. Make a T-table to predict how many dots will be needed for the 6ᵗʰ figure.

Figure 1   Figure 2   Figure 3

5. Jane runs for 10 minutes on Monday.
    Each day she trains for 2 minutes longer.
    How many minutes in all did she run in the first four days?

1. Use addition or multiplication to complete the following charts.
   REMEMBER: There are 60 seconds in a minute, 52 weeks in a year, and 365 days in a year.

a)

Minutes	Seconds
1	60
2	
3	
4	
5	

b)

Years	Weeks
1	52
2	
3	
4	

c)

Years	Days
1	365
2	
3	
4	

2. There are 12 months in a year.
   How many months are there in 4 years?

3. A rabbit's heart beats 200 times a minute.
   How many times will it beat in 5 minutes?

4. A blue goose can fly 1500 km in 2 days.
   How far can it fly in 6 days?

5. Miguel earns $18 for the first hour he works.
   He earns $16 for each hour after that.
   How much will he earn for 5 hours of work?

6. Halley's comet returns to Earth every 76 years. It was last seen in 1986.
   List the next three dates it will return to Earth.

7. Use multiplication or a calculator to find the first few products. Look for a pattern.
   Use the pattern to fill in the rest of the numbers.

a)   999 × 2 = _____   b)   6 × 9 = _____

       999 × 3 = _____   6 × 99 = _____

       999 × 4 = _____   6 × 999 = _____

       _____ = _____   _____ = _____

       _____ = _____   _____ = _____

BONUS

8. Using a calculator, can you discover any patterns like the ones in Question 7?

1. Some apples are inside a box and some are outside. The total number of apples is shown.
   Draw the missing apples in the box.

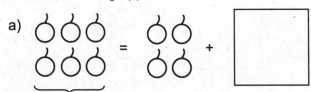

a) 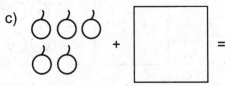 = 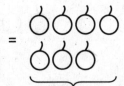 +

total number of apples

b)

c)

total number of apples

d)

2. Draw the missing apples in the box given. Then write an equation (with numbers) to represent the picture.

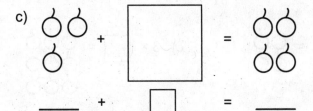

a)

__6__ = __4__ + [2]

b)

____ = ____ + ☐

c)

____ + ☐ = ____

d)

____ + ☐ = ____

3. Write an equation for each situation. (Use a box to stand for the unknown quantity.)

   a) There are 8 apples altogether.
      Six are outside of a box.
      How many are inside?

      8 = 6 + ☐

   b) There are 10 apples altogether.
      4 are outside of a box.
      How many are inside?

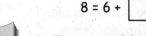

   c) There are 9 balls altogether.
      4 are outside a bag.
      How many are inside?

   d) 5 children are in a tree.
      3 are inside a treehouse.
      How many are outside?

   e) There are 7 children in a park.
      2 are in the pool.
      How many are out of the pool?

   f) Rena has 10 stamps.
      4 are Canadian.
      How many are from other
      countries?

   g) 12 kids are in a class.
      5 are girls.
      How many are boys?

   h) A hockey line has 5 players.
      3 play forward.
      How many play defense?

Patterns & Algebra 2

1. Sam took some apples from a box. Show how many apples were in the box originally.

a)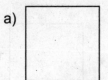

Sam took away this many.   This many were left.

b)

c)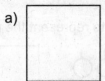

d)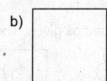

2. Show how many apples were in the box originally. Then write an equation to represent the picture.

a)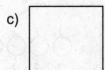

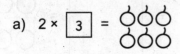

b)

3. In the equations below, 2 × ☐ is a short form for two identical boxes. Show how many apples are in each box.

a) 2 × 3 =

b) 2 × ☐ =

c) 3 × ☐ =

d) 3 × ☐ =

e) 4 × ☐ =

f) 2 × ☐ =

4. Write an equation for each situation.

a) Tom took 3 apples from a box.
2 apples were left.
How many apples were in the box?

b) Sarah took 3 eggs from a carton.
5 eggs were left.
How many eggs were in the carton?

c) Ed has 15 apples in 3 boxes.
Each box contains the same number of apples.
How many apples are in each box?

5. Write a problem to match each equation.

a) ☐ + 2 = 5

b) ☐ − 4 = 6

c) 3 × ☐ = 12

PA4-32: Algebra (Advanced)

1. Find the number that makes the equation true (by guessing and checking) and write it in the box.

   a) ☐ + 2 = 7   b) ☐ + 2 = 8   c) ☐ + 2 = 10   d) ☐ + 5 = 9

   e) 9 – ☐ = 6   f) ☐ – 2 = 7   g) 17 – ☐ = 15   h) 8 – ☐ = 2

   i) 2 × ☐ = 10   j) 5 × ☐ = 15   k) 3 × ☐ = 12

   NOTE: In l), m), and n) below, the two boxes in each question will contain the same number.

   l) ☐ + ☐ = 8   m) ☐ + ☐ = 6   n) ☐ + ☐ + 3 = 13

2. Find a set of numbers that make the equation true. All questions have more than one answer.
   NOTE: In a given question, the same shape represents the same number.

   a) ☐ + ☐ + ◯ = 7   b) ☐ + ☐ + ◯ = 8

3. Find two different answers for the equation below.

   ☐ + ☐ + ◯ = 5   ☐ + ☐ + ◯ = 5

4. Complete the patterns.

   a) 10 + [1] = ◯   b) 10 – [1] = ◯   c) 10 × [1] = ◯

      10 + [2] = ◯   10 – [2] = ◯   10 × [2] = ◯

      10 + [3] = ◯   10 – ☐ = ◯   10 × ☐ = ◯

      10 + ☐ = ◯   10 – ☐ = ◯   10 × ☐ = ◯

5. For each pattern in Question 4, describe how the number in the circle changes as the number in the box increases by one.

6.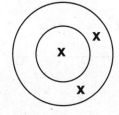
   Paul threw 3 darts and scored 8 points.
   The dart in the centre ring is worth more than the others.
   Each dart in the outer ring is worth more than one point.

   How much is each dart worth?

   HINT: How can an equation like the one in Question 2 b) help you to solve the problem?

jump math
MULTIPLYING POTENTIAL

Patterns & Algebra 2

Show your work for the questions below in your notebook.

1.

    Figure 1   **Figure 2**   **Figure 3**

    How many triangles will be needed for the 6th figure?

2. Sue makes ornaments using squares and triangles.
    She has 12 squares.

    a) How many triangles will she need to use to make
        ornaments with all 12 squares?

    b) How did you solve the problem? Did you use a T-table? A picture? A model?

3.  Hank has to climb 7 walls in an obstacle course.
    The first wall is 200 metres from the start.
    After that, each wall is 50 metres further than the last.
    How far from the start is the 5th wall?

4. Continue the patterns.

    a) 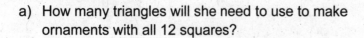 ____ ____

    b) K Q A 10 K Q A ____ ____ ____

    c) 001, 010, 100, 001, ____ , ____ , ____

    d) 000, 001, 011, 111, 000, ____ , ____ , ____

    e) 010, 020, 030, 010, ____ , ____ , ____

    f) AA, AB, AC, AD, ____ , ____ , ____ , ____

    g) M O M M O M M O M ____ ____ ____

    h) 2 T 22 T 222 ____ ____ ____ ____ ____

5. What strategy would you use to find the 23rd shape in this pattern? What is the shape?

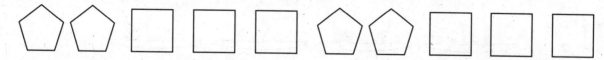

6. Find the mystery number.

a) I am greater than 21 and less than 26. I am a multiple of 3. What am I?

b) I am greater than 29 and less than 33. I am a multiple of 4. What am I?

c) I am less than 15. I am a multiple of 3 <u>and</u> a multiple of 4. What am I?

7. Extend each pattern.

a) 3427 , 3527 , 3627 , _____ , _____ , _____

b) 4234 , 5235 , 6236 , _____ , _____ , _____

c) 1234 , 2345 , 3456 , _____ , _____ , _____

8. Sam and Kiana run up 12 steps with muddy shoes.

a) Sam steps on every 3rd step and Kiana steps on every 4th step. Which steps have both of their footprints on them?

b) If Sam's right foot lands on the 3rd step, on which steps does his left foot land?

9. Every 2nd person who arrives at a book sale receives a free pen. Every 3rd person receives a free book.

Which of the first 15 people will receive a free pen <u>and</u> book?

10. Emma makes a staircase using stone blocks.

How many blocks will she need to build a stairway 6 steps high?

  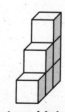

1 step high   2 steps high   3 steps high

Elisa has 12 glasses of water. A tray holds 3 glasses.

There are 4 trays.

What has been shared or divided into <u>sets</u> or <u>groups</u>?   *(Glasses)*

How many sets are there?   *(There are 4 sets of glasses.)*

How many of the things being divided are in each set?   *(There are 3 glasses in each set.)*

---

1. a)

    What has been shared or divided into sets?

    _____

    How many sets? _____

    How many in each set? _____

    b)

    What has been shared or divided into sets?

    _____

    How many sets? _____

    How many in each set? _____

2. Using circles for <u>sets</u> and dots for <u>things</u>, draw a picture to show…

    a) 4 sets
        6 things in each set

    b) 6 groups
        3 things in each group

    c) 6 sets
        2 things in each set

    d) 4 groups
        5 things in each group

3.

	What has been shared or divided into sets?	How many sets?	How many in each set?

a) 20 toys
   4 toys for each child
   5 kids
	20 toys	5	4

b) 7 friends
   21 pencils
   3 pencils for each friend			

c) 16 students
   4 desks
   4 students at each desk			

d) 8 plants
   24 flowers
   3 flowers on each plant			

e) 6 grapefruits in each box
   42 grapefruits
   7 boxes			

f) 3 school buses
   30 children
   10 children in each school bus			

g) 6 puppies in each litter
   6 litters
   36 puppies			

BONUS

4. Draw a picture for Questions 3 a), b), and c) using <u>circles</u> for sets and <u>dots</u> for the things being divided.

Kate wants to share 16 cookies with three friends.
She sets out four plates (one for herself and one for each of her friends).

She puts one cookie at
a time on the plates:

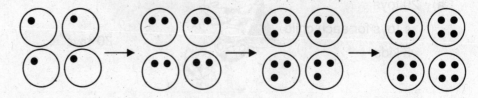

Each plate holds a **set** (or group) of 4 cookies.
When 16 cookies are **divided** (or shared equally) into 4 sets, there are 4 cookies **in each set**.

----

1. Put an equal number of cookies on each plate. Draw circles for the plates and dots for the cookies.
   (Draw the plates, then place one cookie at a time.)

   a) 12 cookies; 3 plates

   b) 16 cookies; 4 plates

2. Draw dots for the things being shared or divided equally. Draw circles for the sets.

   a) 2 vans; 8 people
      How many people in each van?

   b) 3 kids; 9 stickers
      How many stickers for each kid?

   c) 20 flowers; 5 plants
      How many flowers on each plant?

   d) 12 grapefruits; 6 boxes
      How many grapefruits in each box?

3. 5 friends shared 20 cherries equally. How many cherries does each friend get?

4. Eileen shared 12 stickers among 3 friends and herself. How many stickers does each person get?

5. There are 16 apples in 8 trees. How many apples are in each tree?

Saud has 30 apples. He wants to give 5 apples to each of his friends.

To find out how many friends he can give apples to, he counts out **sets** or **groups** of 5 apples until he has used all 30 apples.

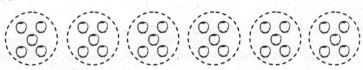

He can give apples to 6 friends. When 30 apples are divided into sets of 5 apples, there are 6 sets.

----

1. Put the correct number of dots in each set. The first one has been done for you.

a)   b)    c)

    4 dots in each set   5 dots in each set   3 dots in each set

2. Draw circles to divide these arrays into …

a) groups of 3   b) groups of 4   c) groups of 3   d) groups of 4

     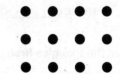      

3. Draw dots for the things being shared or divided equally. Draw circles for the sets.

a) 15 apples; 5 apples in each box.
    How many boxes?

b) 10 stickers; 2 stickers for each kid.
    How many kids?

_____ boxes   _____ kids

 4. Shelly has 18 cookies. She gives 3 cookies to each of her siblings.
     How many siblings does she have?

5. Vinaya has 14 stamps. He puts 2 stamps on each envelope.
    How many envelopes does he have?

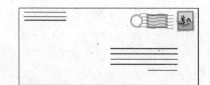

Samuel has 15 cookies. There are two ways he can share or <u>divide</u> his cookies equally:

I • He can decide how many <u>sets</u> (or <u>groups</u>) of cookies he wants to make.

For example:

Samuel wants to make 3 sets of cookies. He draws 3 circles:

He puts one cookie at a time into the circles until he has placed 15 cookies.

II • He can decide how many cookies he wants to put <u>in each set</u>.

For example:

Samuel wants to put 5 cookies in each set. He counts out 5 cookies:

He counts out sets of 5 cookies until he has placed 15 cookies in sets.

- -

1. Share **20** dots equally. How many dots are in each set? **HINT: Place one dot at a time.**

    a) 4 sets:

    There are _____ dots in each set.

    b) 5 sets:

    There are _____ dots in each set.

2. Share the triangles equally among the sets. **HINT: Count the triangles first.**

    a)

    b)

3. Share the squares equally among the sets.

4. Group the lines so that there are 3 lines in each set.

    a) | | | | | | | | |

    b) | | | | | | | | | | | |

    c) | | | | | |

    There are _____ sets.

    There are _____ sets.

    There are _____ sets.

5. Group **12** dots so that…

    a) there are 6 dots in each set.

    b) there are 4 dots in each set.

6. In each question fill in what you know. Write a question mark for what you don't know.

	What has been shared or divided into sets?	How many sets?	How many in each set?
a) Vanessa has 25 pencils. She puts 5 pencils in each box.	25 pencils	?	5
b) 30 children are in 10 boats.	30 children	10	?
c) Ben has 36 stickers. He gives 9 stickers to each of his friends.			
d) Donald has 12 books. He puts 3 on each shelf.			
e) 15 girls sit at 3 tables.			
f) 30 students are in 2 school buses.			
g) 9 fruit bars are shared among 3 children.			
h) 15 chairs are in 3 rows.			
i) Each basket holds 4 eggs. There are 12 eggs altogether.			

7. Draw a picture using dots and circles to solve each question.

a) 15 dots; 5 sets

_____ dots in each set

b) 16 dots; 8 dots in each set

_____ sets

c) 15 dots; 5 dots in each set

_____ sets

d) 8 dots; 4 sets

_____ dots in each set

e) 10 children are in 2 boats.

How many children are in each boat? _____

f) Paul has 12 pencils.
   He puts 3 pencils in each box.

How many boxes does he have? _____

g) 4 boys share 12 marbles.

How many marbles does each boy get? _____

h) Pamela has 10 apples.
   She gives 2 apples to each friend.

How many friends receive apples? _____

i) 6 children go sailing in 2 boats.

How many children are in each boat? _____

j) Alan has 10 stickers.
   He puts 2 on each page.

How many pages does he use? _____

Every **division** statement implies an **addition** statement.

For example, the statement "15 divided into sets of size 3 gives 5 sets" is equivalent to the statement "adding 3 five times gives 15".

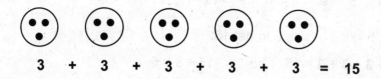

3 + 3 + 3 + 3 + 3 = 15

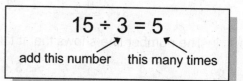

$$15 \div 3 = 5$$

add this number   this many times

Hence the division statement $15 \div 3 = 5$ can be read as "add three five times."

---

1. Draw a picture and write an <u>addition</u> statement for each <u>division</u> statement, as shown in a).

   a) $8 \div 2 = 4$ b) $10 \div 5 = 2$ c) $8 \div 4 = 2$

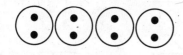

$\underline{\quad 2 + 2 + 2 + 2 = 8 \quad}$ _____   _____

2. Draw a picture and write a <u>division</u> statement for each <u>addition</u> statement.

   a) $4 + 4 + 4 = 12$ b) $7 + 7 + 7 = 21$

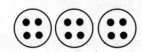

$\underline{\quad 12 \div 4 = 3 \quad}$ _____

   c) $6 + 6 + 6 = 18$ d) $8 + 8 = 16$

_____   _____

   e) $3 + 3 + 3 + 3 = 12$ f) $9 + 9 = 18$

_____   _____

NS4-57: Dividing by Skip Counting

1. You can solve the division problem **15 ÷ 3 = ?** by skip counting on the number line.

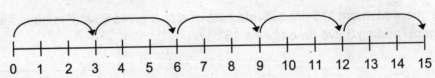

The number line shows that it takes 5 skips of size 3 to get 15:

$$3 + 3 + 3 + 3 + 3 = 15 \quad so ... \quad 15 ÷ 3 = 5$$

Use the number line to find the answer to the division statement. (Draw arrows to show your skip counting.)

a)

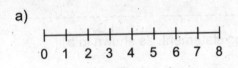

8 ÷ 2 = _____

b)

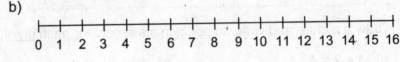

16 ÷ 8 = _____

2. What division statement does the picture represent?

a)

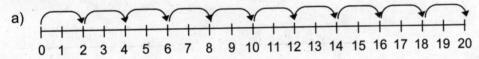

_____

b)

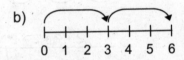

_____

3. You can also find the answer to a division question by skip counting on your fingers.

   Example: To find **45 ÷ 9** skip count by 9s until you reach 45

   The number of fingers you have up when you stop is the answer.

   45 ÷ 9   18   27   36   45   **So 45 ÷ 9 = 5**

   Find the answers by skip counting on your fingers.

   a) 14 ÷ 2 = _____   b) 18 ÷ 6 = _____   c) 24 ÷ 8 = _____   d) 21 ÷ 7 = _____   e) 35 ÷ 5 = _____

   f) 45 ÷ 5 = _____   g) 32 ÷ 4 = _____   h) 40 ÷ 5 = _____   i) 24 ÷ 3 = _____   j) 16 ÷ 4 = _____

   k) 36 ÷ 9 = _____   l) 28 ÷ 7 = _____   m) 12 ÷ 3 = _____   n) 18 ÷ 3 = _____   o) 35 ÷ 7 = _____

4. Seven friends share 28 tickets to a concert. How many tickets does each friend get?

5. 30 students sit in 6 rows. How many students are in each row?

Number Sense 2

Daniel bought 12 fish from a pet store: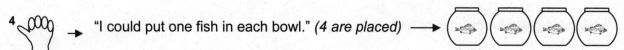

Daniel has 4 fish bowls. How many fish can he put in each fish bowl? Daniel counts by 4s to find out:

 "I could put one fish in each bowl." *(4 are placed)* →

 "I could put one more in each bowl." *(8 are placed)* →

 "I could put one more in each bowl." *(12 are placed)* →

He has raised 3 fingers, so he knows that **12 ÷ 4 = 3**. He puts 3 fish in each fish bowl.

----

1. Draw circles to divide the objects into the number of sets given.
   HINT: Divide the number of objects by the number of sets to find the number of objects in each set.

   a) | | | | | | | | | | | |

   3 equal sets

   b) ♡ ♡ ♡ ♡ ♡ ♡ ♡ ♡ ♡ ♡

   5 equal sets

   c) ✦ ✦ ✦ ✦ ✦ ✦ ✦ ✦

   2 equal sets

   d) ✵ ✵ ✵ ✵ ✵ ✵ ✵ ✵ ✵ ✵ ✵ ✵

   4 equal sets

   e) ● ● ● ● ● ● ● ● ● ● ● ● ● ●

   7 equal sets

   f) ◻◻◻◻◻◻◻◻◻◻◻◻◻◻

   2 equal sets

   g) ◇ ◇ ◇ ◇ ◇ ◇ ◇ ◇ ◇ ◇ ◇ ◇

   3 equal sets

   h) ○○○○○○○○○○○○

   6 equal sets

   BONUS

   i)

   3 equal sets

   j)

   5 equal sets

   k)

   4 equal sets

2. Azul has 16 fish and 4 fish bowls. How many fish can he put in each bowl?

   Write a division statement for your answer. _____

When 15 things are divided into 5 sets, there are 3 things in each set: **15 ÷ 5 = 3**

We could also describe the picture as follows.

When 15 things are divided into sets of size 3, there are 5 sets: **15 ÷ 3 = 5**

---

3. Fill in the blanks. Then write two division statements.

a)

_____ lines   _____ sets

_____ lines in each set

_____ ÷ _____ = _____

_____ ÷ _____ = _____

b)

_____ lines   _____ sets

_____ lines in each set

_____

_____

c)

_____ lines   _____ sets

_____ lines in each set

_____

_____

4. Fill in the blanks. Then write two division statements.
    HINT: Count the figures first.

a)

_____ sets

_____ squares in each set

_____

_____

b)

_____ sets

_____ triangles in each set

_____

_____

c)

_____ sets

_____ stars in each set

_____

_____

5. Solve the problem by drawing a picture. Then write a division statement for your answer.

a) 12 triangles; 4 sets

_____

How many triangles in each set? _____

b) 6 squares; 3 squares in each set

_____

How many sets? _____

6. Solve each problem by drawing a picture. Write a division statement for your answer.

a) 20 people; 5 cars
    How many people in each car?

b) 12 children; 3 boats
    How many children in each boat?

Every **division** statement implies a **multiplication** statement. The statement:

"10 divided into sets of size 2 gives 5 sets" (or **10 ÷ 2 = 5**)

can be rewritten as "5 sets of size 2 equals 10" (**5 × 2 = 10**).

REMEMBER: 10 ÷ 2 = 5 implies 10 ÷ 5 = 2 and 5 × 2 = 10 implies 2 × 5 = 10.

- -

1. Write two multiplication statements and two division statements for each picture.

a)

_____

_____

_____

b)

_____

_____

_____

c)

_____

_____

_____

How many fish? _____

How many sets? _____

How many fish in each set? _____

d)

_____

_____

_____

How many snails? _____

How many sets? _____

How many snails in each set? _____

2. Find the answer to the division problem by first finding the answer to the multiplication statement.

a) 4 × $\boxed{5}$ = 20

20 ÷ 4 = $\boxed{5}$

b) 6 × $\square$ = 12

12 ÷ 6 = $\square$

c) 5 × $\square$ = 20

20 ÷ 5 = $\square$

d) 6 × $\square$ = 30

30 ÷ 6 = $\square$

e) 9 × $\square$ = 45

45 ÷ 9 = $\square$

f) 7 × $\square$ = 21

21 ÷ 7 = $\square$

g) 3 × $\square$ = 24

24 ÷ 3 = $\square$

h) 6 × $\square$ = 24

24 ÷ 6 = $\square$

TEACHER:
To solve word problems involving multiplication or division, students should ask:

- How many things are there altogether?
- How many things are in each set?
- How many sets or groups are there?

Your students should also know (and be able to explain using pictures or concrete materials):

- When you know the number of sets and the number of things in each set, you multiply to find the total number of things.

- When you know the total number of things and the number of sets, you divide to find the number of things in each set.

- When you know the total number of things and the number of things in each set, you divide to find the number of sets.

---

1. For each picture, fill in the blanks.

a)

_____ lines

_____ lines in each set

_____ sets

b)

_____ lines in total

_____ groups

_____ lines in each set

c)

_____ lines in each set

_____ groups

_____ lines altogether

d)

_____ lines in each set

_____ sets

_____ lines altogether

e)

_____ lines

_____ lines in each set

_____ sets

f)

_____ lines in total

_____ groups

_____ lines in each group

2. Draw a picture of …
   a) 16 lines altogether; 4 lines in each set; 4 sets
   b) 8 lines; 4 lines in each set; 2 sets
   c) 6 sets; 3 lines in each set; 18 lines in total
   d) 12 lines; 2 sets; 6 lines in each set

3. Draw a picture of <u>and</u> write two division statements and a multiplication statement for …
   a) 20 lines; 5 sets; 4 lines in each set
   b) 15 lines; 5 lines in each set; 3 sets

1. In each question below some information is missing (indicated by a question mark).
   Write a multiplication or division statement to find the missing information.

	Total number of things	Number of sets	Number in each set	Multiplication or division statement
a)	?	6	3	6 × 3 = 18
b)	20	4	?	20 ÷ 4 = 5
c)	15	?	5	
d)	10	2	?	
e)	?	4	6	
f)	21	7	?	

2. For each question, write a multiplication or a division statement to solve the problem.

a) 18 things in total
   3 things in each set

   _____18 ÷ 3 = 6_____

   How many sets?

   _____6_____

b) 5 sets
   4 things in each set

   _____

   How many things in total?

   _____

c) 15 things in total
   5 sets

   _____

   How many things in each set?

   _____

d) 8 groups
   3 things in each group

   _____

   How many things in total?

   _____

e) 6 things in each set
   12 things in total

   _____

   How many sets?

   _____

f) 5 groups
   10 things in total

   _____

   How many in each group?

   _____

g) 5 things in each set
   4 sets

   _____

   How many things in total?

   _____

h) 4 things in each set
   6 sets

   _____

   How many things in total?

   _____

i) 16 things in total
   8 sets

   _____

   How many things in each set?

   _____

3. Fill in the chart. Use a question mark to show what you don't know. Then write a multiplication or division statement in the right hand column.

	Total Number of things	Number of sets	Number in each set	Multiplication or division statement
a) 20 people 4 vans	20	4	?	20 ÷ 4 = 5 How many people in each van? _____5_____
b) 3 marbles in each jar 6 jars				How many marbles? _____
c) 15 flowers 5 pots				How many flowers in each pot? _____
d) 4 chairs at each table 2 tables				How many chairs? _____
e) 18 pillows 6 beds				How many pillows on each bed? _____
f) 18 houses 9 houses on each block				How many blocks? _____

4. The fact family for the multiplication statement **3 × 5 = 15** is: **5 × 3 = 15; 15 ÷ 3 = 5 and 15 ÷ 5 = 3**. Write the fact family of equations for the following statements.

a) 5 × 2 = 10   b) 4 × 3 = 12   c) 8 × 4 = 32   d) 9 × 3 = 27

NS4-62: Remainders

Ori wants to share 7 strawberries with 2 friends.

He sets out 3 plates, one for himself and one for each of his friends.

He puts one strawberry at a time on a plate:

There is one strawberry left over.

7 strawberries cannot be shared equally into 3 sets. Each friend gets 2 strawberries, but one is left over.

7 ÷ 3 = 2 Remainder 1

- -

1. Can you share 5 strawberries equally onto 2 plates? Show your work using dots and circles.

2. Share the dots as equally as possible among the circles.

   IMPORTANT: In one question, the dots can be shared equally (so there's no remainder).

   a) 7 dots in 2 circles

   _____ dots in each circle; _____ dot remaining

   b) 10 dots in 3 circles

   _____ dots in each circle; _____ dot remaining

   c) 10 dots in 5 circles

   _____ dots in each circle; _____ dots remaining

   d) 9 dots in 4 circles

   _____ dots in each circle; _____ dot remaining

   e) 12 dots in 5 circles

   _____ dots in each circle; _____ dots remaining

   f) 13 dots in 4 circles

   _____ dots in each circle; _____ dot remaining

Number Sense 2

NS4-62: Remainders (continued)

3. Share the dots as equally as possible. Draw a picture and write a division statement.

a) 7 dots in 3 circles	b) 11 dots in 3 circles

$$7 \div 3 = 2 \text{ Remainder } 1$$

c) 14 dots in 3 circles	d) 10 dots in 6 circles
e) 10 dots in 4 circles	f) 13 dots in 5 circles

4. Three friends want to share 7 cherries. How many cherries will each friend receive? How many will be left over? Show your work and write a division statement.

5. Find two different ways to share 13 granola bars into equal groups so that one is left over.

6. Fred, George and Paul have less than 10 oranges and more than 3 oranges. They share the oranges evenly. How many oranges do they have? Is there more than one answer?

Paul has 14 oranges. He wants to give a bag of 4 oranges to each of his friends.

He skip counts to find out how many friends
he can share with.

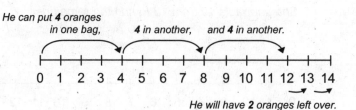

*He can put **4** oranges
in one bag,*   ***4** in another,*   *and **4** in another.*

0 1 2 3 4 5 6 7 8 9 10 11 12 13 14

*He will have **2** oranges left over.*

14 oranges divided into sets of size 4
gives 3 sets (with 2 oranges **remaining**):

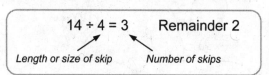

14 ÷ 4 = 3   Remainder 2

Length or size of skip   *Number of skips*

---

1. Fill in the missing numbers. For parts d) and e), write a division statement.

a)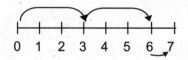

0 1 2 3 4 5 6 7

Size of skip = _____   Number of skips = _____

Remainder = _____

b)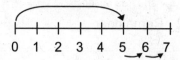

0 1 2 3 4 5 6 7

Size of skip = _____   Number of skips = _____

Remainder = _____

c) Size of skip = _____

Number of skips = _____

Remainder = _____

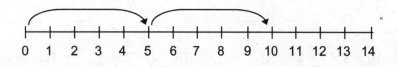

0 1 2 3 4 5 6 7 8 9 10 11 12 13 14

d)

0 1 2 3 4 5 6 7 8 9 10

Size of skip = _____   Number of skips = _____

Remainder = _____

_____

e)

0 1 2 3 4 5 6 7 8

Size of skip = _____   Number of skips = _____

Remainder = _____

_____

2. Jane has 11 oranges. She wants to make bags of 4.
   How many bags can she make?
   How many oranges will be left over?

0 1 2 3 4 5 6 7 8 9 10 11

3. On grid paper, draw a number line picture to model the division.

a) 5 ÷ 2 = 2 Remainder 1   b) 9 ÷ 4 = 2 Remainder 1   c) 11 ÷ 3 = 3 Remainder 2

Number Sense 2

Nina wants to find 13 ÷ 5 mentally.

Step 1:
Counting by 5s, she raises two fingers (she stops before she reaches 13).

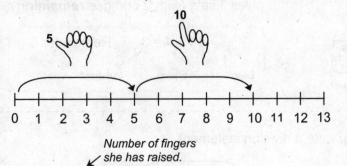

Number of fingers she has raised.

13 ÷ 5 = _2_ Remainder ___

Step 2:
Nina stopped counting at 10.
She subtracts 10 from 13 to find the remainder.

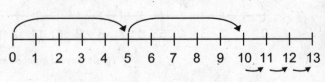

13 ÷ 5 = _2_ Remainder _3_

1. Try to answer the following questions in your head (or by skip counting).

   a) 18 ÷ 5 = _____ R _____   b) 23 ÷ 5 = _____ R _____   c) 26 ÷ 5 = _____ R _____

   d) 28 ÷ 5 = _____ R _____   e) 16 ÷ 5 = _____ R _____   f) 6 ÷ 5 = _____ R _____

   g) 10 ÷ 3 = _____ R _____   h) 7 ÷ 3 = _____ R _____   i) 16 ÷ 3 = _____ R _____

   j) 8 ÷ 2 = _____ R _____   k) 5 ÷ 2 = _____ R _____   l) 17 ÷ 4 = _____ R _____

   m) 16 ÷ 7 = _____ R _____   n) 28 ÷ 9 = _____ R _____   o) 25 ÷ 8 = _____ R _____

   p) 13 ÷ 2 = _____ R _____   q) 45 ÷ 8 = _____ R _____   r) 63 ÷ 7 = _____ R _____

2. Richard wants to divide 16 pencils between 5 friends.

   How many pencils will each friend get? _____

   How many will be left over? _____

3. You have 17 tickets to a school play-day.
   You want to give 5 tickets to each friend.

   How many friends can you share with? _____

   How many tickets will be left over? _____

NS4-65: Long Division — 2-Digit by 1-Digit

Inez is preparing snacks for 4 classes. She needs to divide 93 apples into 4 groups.

She will use long division and a model to solve the problem.

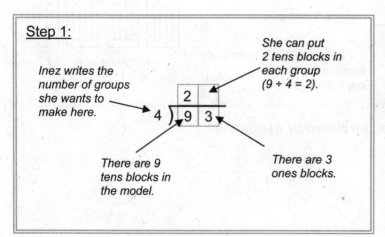

Step 1:

Inez writes the number of groups she wants to make here.

She can put 2 tens blocks in each group (9 ÷ 4 = 2).

There are 9 tens blocks in the model.

There are 3 ones blocks.

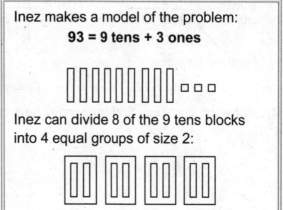

Inez makes a model of the problem:
93 = 9 tens + 3 ones

Inez can divide 8 of the 9 tens blocks into 4 equal groups of size 2:

---

1. Inez has written a division statement to solve a problem. How many groups does she want to make? How many tens blocks and how many ones would she need to model the problem?

   a) $3 \overline{)85}$

   groups ___3___

   tens blocks ___8___

   ones ___5___

   b) $4 \overline{)92}$

   groups _____

   tens blocks _____

   ones _____

   c) $5 \overline{)86}$

   groups _____

   tens blocks _____

   ones _____

   d) $2 \overline{)87}$

   groups _____

   tens blocks _____

   ones _____

2. How many tens blocks can be put in each group? Use division or skip counting to find the answers.

   a) $3 \overline{)\boxed{7}\,5}$ with $\boxed{2}$ on top

   b) $4 \overline{)\boxed{9}\,3}$

   c) $5 \overline{)\boxed{6}\,2}$

   d) $3 \overline{)\boxed{9}\,8}$

   e) $4 \overline{)\boxed{8}\,2}$

   f) $2 \overline{)\boxed{8}\,5}$

   g) $3 \overline{)\boxed{8}\,7}$

   h) $8 \overline{)\boxed{9}\,1}$

   i) $6 \overline{)\boxed{8}\,3}$

   j) $5 \overline{)\boxed{9}\,2}$

3. How many groups have been made? How many tens are in each group?

   a) $3 \overline{)\boxed{7}\,5}$ with $\boxed{2}$ on top

   groups ___3___

   number of tens in each group ___2___

   b) $2 \overline{)\boxed{9}\,1}$

   groups _____

   number of tens in each group _____

   c) $4 \overline{)\boxed{9}\,5}$

   groups _____

   number of tens in each group _____

   d) $2 \overline{)\boxed{7}\,3}$

   groups _____

   number of tens in each group _____

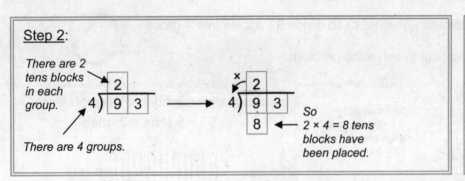

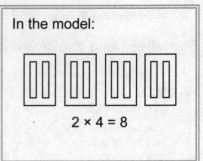

4. For each question, find how many tens can be placed by multiplying?

a)

$$3 \overline{\smash{)}\, 8 \ 7}$$ with 2 above

How many groups? _____

How many tens? _____

How many tens in each group? _____

How many tens placed altogether? _____

b)

$$4 \overline{\smash{)}\, 9 \ 6}$$ with 2 above

How many groups? _____

How many tens? _____

How many tens in each group? _____

How many tens placed altogether? _____

5. Use skip counting to find out how many tens can be placed in each group. Then use multiplication to find out how many tens have been placed.

a) $2 \overline{\smash{)}\, 7 \ 3}$ b) $3 \overline{\smash{)}\, 8 \ 2}$ c) $2 \overline{\smash{)}\, 9 \ 5}$ d) $5 \overline{\smash{)}\, 9 \ 8}$ e) $7 \overline{\smash{)}\, 8 \ 1}$

f) $6 \overline{\smash{)}\, 6 \ 3}$ g) $2 \overline{\smash{)}\, 7 \ 1}$ h) $3 \overline{\smash{)}\, 7 \ 5}$ i) $4 \overline{\smash{)}\, 9 \ 3}$ j) $8 \overline{\smash{)}\, 8 \ 5}$

k) $2 \overline{\smash{)}\, 8 \ 1}$ l) $3 \overline{\smash{)}\, 7 \ 2}$ m) $9 \overline{\smash{)}\, 9 \ 5}$ n) $7 \overline{\smash{)}\, 9 \ 3}$ o) $6 \overline{\smash{)}\, 8 \ 0}$

p) $2 \overline{\smash{)}\, 5 \ 3}$ q) $3 \overline{\smash{)}\, 7 \ 8}$ r) $4 \overline{\smash{)}\, 9 \ 0}$ s) $5 \overline{\smash{)}\, 5 \ 0}$ t) $6 \overline{\smash{)}\, 7 \ 3}$

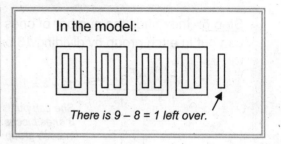

Step 3: *There are 9 tens blocks and Inez has placed 8.*

She subtracts to find out how many are left over (9 − 8 = 1).

In the model:

There is 9 − 8 = 1 left over.

6. For each question, carry out the first three steps of the long division.

a) 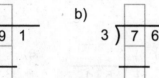 6) 9 1

b) 3) 7 6

c) 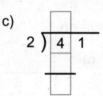 2) 4 1

d) 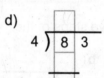 4) 8 3

e) 3) 8 5

f) 4) 5 7

g) 8) 9 3

h) 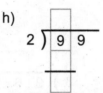 2) 9 9

i) 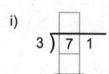 3) 7 1

j) 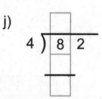 4) 8 2

Step 4: There is one tens block left over and 3 ones. So there are 13 ones left over. Inez writes the 3 beside the 1 to show this.

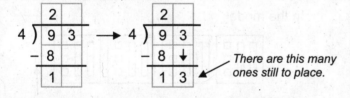

There are this many ones still to place.

In the model:

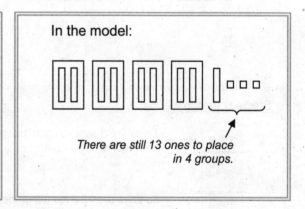

There are still 13 ones to place in 4 groups.

7. Carry out the first four steps of the long division.

a) 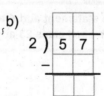 3) 7 5

b) 2) 5 7

c) 2) 9 3

d) 4) 8 3

e) 6) 8 1

f) 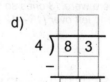 4) 6 3

g) 2) 3 5

h) 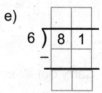 7) 8 8

i) 8) 9 1

j) 9) 9 3

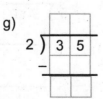 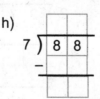 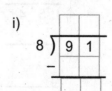 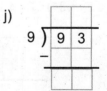

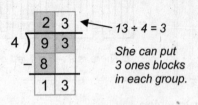

Step 5: Inez finds the number of ones she can put in each group by dividing 13 by 4.

13 ÷ 4 = 3

She can put 3 ones blocks in each group.

In the model:

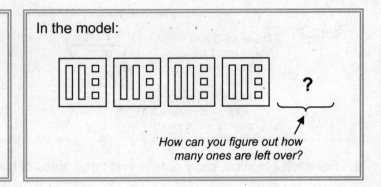

How can you figure out how many ones are left over?

8. Carry out the first five steps of the long division.

a) 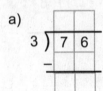 3) 7 6

b)   5) 7 5

c)   2) 5 5

d) 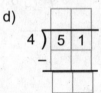 4) 5 1

e) 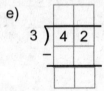 3) 4 2

f) 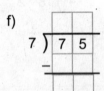 7) 7 5

g) 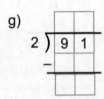 2) 9 1

h) 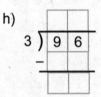 3) 9 6

i) 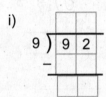 9) 9 2

j) 2) 7 3

Steps 6 and 7:

There are 3 ones in each group... and there are 4 groups.

So there are 12 ones altogether in the groups (3 × 4 = 12).

There were 13 ones so there is 1 one left over (13 − 12 = 1)

In the model:

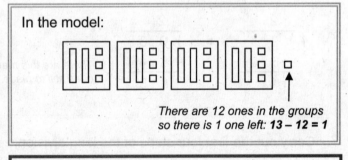

*There are 12 ones in the groups so there is 1 one left: **13 − 12 = 1***

The division statement and the model both show that Inez can give each class 23 apples with one left over.

9. Carry out all seven steps of the long division.

a) 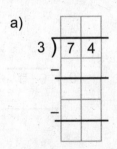 3) 7 4

b) 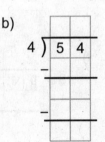 4) 5 4

c) 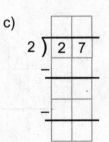 2) 2 7

d) 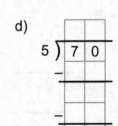 5) 7 0

e) 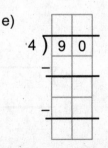 4) 9 0

f)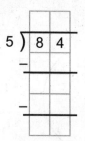
$5 \overline{)84}$

g)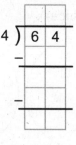
$4 \overline{)64}$

h)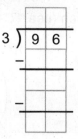
$3 \overline{)96}$

i)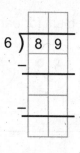
$6 \overline{)89}$

j)
$7 \overline{)97}$

k)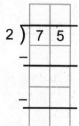
$2 \overline{)75}$

l)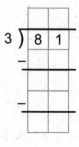
$3 \overline{)81}$

m)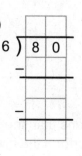
$6 \overline{)80}$

n)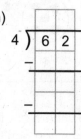
$4 \overline{)62}$

o)
$8 \overline{)97}$

10. Sandra put 62 tomatoes into cartons of 5.
How many tomatoes did she have left over?

11. How many weeks are there in 84 days?

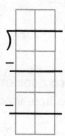

12. A pentagon has a perimeter of 95 cm.
How long is each side?

13. Shawn can hike 8 km in a day.
How many days will it take him to hike 96 km?

14. A boat can hold 6 kids.
How many boats will 84 kids need?

15. Alexa put 73 apples in bags of 6.
Mike put 46 apples in bags of 4.
Who had more apples left over?

NS4-66: Further Division

1. Write a division statement for each question (use "R" for remainder).

a)

_____

b)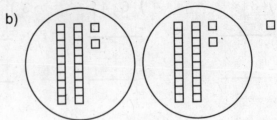

_____

c)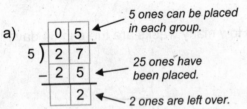

_____

2. In each question below there are fewer tens than the number of groups.
   Write a 0 in the tens position and then perform the division (as if the tens had been regrouped as ones).

a)
```
    0 5   ← 5 ones can be placed
5 ) 2 7      in each group.
  - 2 5   ← 25 ones have
  -------    been placed.
      2   ← 2 ones are left over.
```

b) 5) 3 1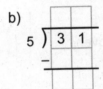

c) 4) 3 3

d) 8) 5 2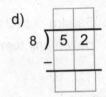

3. Estimate each quotient by first rounding each number to the nearest ten.
   Then find the actual answer by long division.

   a) 87 ÷ 9   b) 78 ÷ 8   c) 91 ÷ 8   d) 126 ÷ 9

4. When you divide a number by 1, what is the result? Explain.

In Questions 5 to 8, you will have to interpret what the remainder means.

5. A canoe can hold 3 kids.
   How many canoes will 44 kids need?

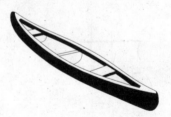

6. Anne reads 5 pages before bed every night.
   She has 63 pages left to read in her book.
   How many nights will it take her to finish her book?

7. Ed wants to give 65 hockey cards to 4 friends.
   How many cards will each friend get?

8. Daniel wants to put 97 hockey cards into a scrap book.
   A page can hold 9 cards.
   How many pages will he need?

NS4-67: Unit Rates

A **rate** is a comparison of two quantities in different units.

In a **unit rate**, one of the quantities is equal to one.

For instance, "1 apple costs 30¢" is a unit rate.

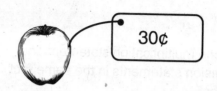

30¢

---

1. Fill in the missing information.

   a) 1 book costs $4

      2 books cost _____

      3 books cost _____

      4 books cost _____

   b) 1 ticket costs 5¢

      2 tickets cost _____

      3 tickets cost _____

      4 tickets cost _____

   c) 1 apple costs 20¢

      2 apples cost _____

      3 apples cost _____

      4 apples cost _____

   d) 20 km in 1 hour

      _____ km in 3 hours

   e) $12 allowance in 1 week

      _____ allowance in 4 weeks

   f) 1 teacher for 25 students

      3 teachers for _____

   g) 1 kg of rice for 10 cups of water   5 kg of rice for _____ cups of water

2. In the pictures, 1 centimetre represents 3 metres. Use a ruler to find out how long each whale is.

Length in cm _____

Length in m _____

Killer Whale

Length in cm _____

Length in m _____

Bowhead Whale

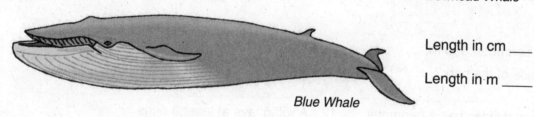

Length in cm _____

Length in m _____

Blue Whale

3. Cho earns $8 an hour babysitting. How much will he earn in 4 hours?

4. Alice earns $10 an hour mowing lawns. How much will she earn in 8 hours?

5. Find the unit rate.

   a) 2 books cost $10

      1 book costs _____.

   b) 4 mangoes cost $12

      1 mango costs _____.

   c) 6 cans of juice cost $12

      1 can costs _____.

NS4-68: Concepts in Multiplication and Division

Answer the following questions in your notebook.

1. Write one multiplication statement and two division statements in the same fact family as …

$$6 \times 8 = 48$$

2. Find the mystery numbers.

   a) I am a multiple of 4. I am greater than 25 and less than 31.

   b) I am divisible by 3. I am between 20 and 26. I am an even number.

3. 92 kids attend a play on 4 buses. There are an equal number of kids on each bus.

   a) How many kids are on each bus?

   b) A ticket for the play costs $6. How much will it cost for one busload of kids to attend the play?

4. Find two different ways to share 14 apples in equal groups so there are 2 apples left over.

   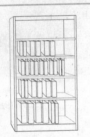

5. Find three numbers that give the same remainder when divided by 3.

6. A queen ant can lay one egg every ten seconds. How many eggs can she lay in…

   a) 1 minute?   b) 2 minutes?   c) an hour?

   How did you find your answers?

7. Six friends read 96 books for a read-a-thon.

   Each friend reads the same number of books.

   How many books did each friend read?

8. Jennifer plants 84 pansies in 4 flower beds. How many pansies are in each flower bed?

9. A square park has perimeter 680 m.

   How long is each side of the park?

10. A square park has sides of length 236 m.

    What is the perimeter of the park?

11. A pentagon with equal sides has a perimeter of 75 cm.

    How long is each side?

    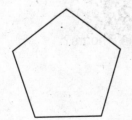

12. A robin lays <u>at least</u> 3 eggs and <u>no more than</u> 6 eggs.

    a) What is the least number of eggs 3 robins' nests would hold (if there were eggs laid in each nest)?

    b) What is the greatest number of eggs 3 robins' nests would hold?

    c) Three robins' nests contain 13 eggs.

       Draw a picture to show 2 ways the eggs could be shared among the nests.

1. Pick two numbers, one from each of the boxes to the right, so that ...

   a) the product of the two numbers is smallest: _____ × _____ = _____

   b) the product is the greatest: _____ × _____ = _____

   c) the product is closest to 20: _____ × _____ = _____

   d) the difference between the numbers is smallest: _____ – _____ = _____

2. Show all the ways you can colour the flag with red (R), green (G), and blue (B) using one stripe of each colour.

3. Using the numbered boxes below, show all the ways you can make a stack of <u>two</u> boxes so that a box with a lower number never sits on top of a box with a higher number.

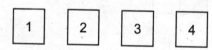

4. Crayons come in boxes of 4 or 5. Can you buy a combination of boxes that contain ...
   NOTE: For some of these questions, you needn't buy boxes of both types. Show your work.

   a) 8 crayons?   b) 10 crayons?   c) 11 crayons?   d) 14 crayons?

   e) 17 crayons?   f) 18 crayons?   g) 19 crayons?   h) 21 crayons?

BONUS

5. A frog takes two long jumps (of equal length) and two shorter jumps (of equal length).

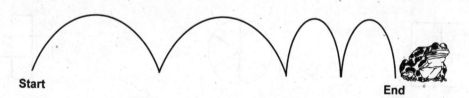

   What lengths could the first and last jumps be if the frog jumps a total distance of ...

   a) 10 metres?   ├┼┼┼┼┼┼┼┼┼┤   first: _____ m   last: _____ m

   b) 16 metres?   ├┼┼┼┼┼┼┼┼┼┼┼┼┼┼┼┤   first: _____ m   last: _____ m

NS4-70: Naming of Fractions

The pie is cut into 4 equal parts.

3 parts out of 4 are shaded.

$\frac{3}{4}$ of a pie is shaded.

$\frac{3}{4}$

*The **numerator** (3) tells you how many parts are counted.*

*The **denominator** (4) tells you how many parts in a whole.*

---

1. Name the fraction shown by the shaded part of each image.

a)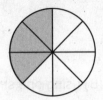

b)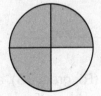

c)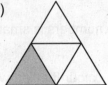

d)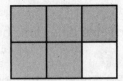

e)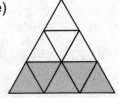

f)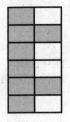

g)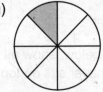

h)

2. Shade the fractions named.

a) $\frac{3}{6}$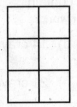

b) $\frac{2}{5}$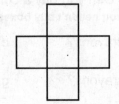

c) $\frac{5}{9}$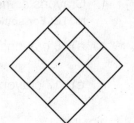

3. Use one of the following words to describe the parts in the figures below.

halves   thirds   fourths   fifths   sixths   sevenths   eighths   ninths

a)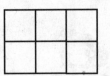

b)

c)

d)

e)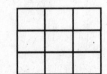

f)

1. Use a **ruler** to divide each line into equal parts.

   a) 5 equal parts

   b) 3 equal parts

   c) 4 equal parts

   _____

   _____

   _____

   d) 7 equal parts

   e) 9 equal parts

   _____

   _____

2. Use a **ruler** to divide each box into equal parts.

   a) 4 equal parts

   b) 5 equal parts

   c) 3 equal parts

   d) 6 equal parts

3. Using a **ruler**, find what fraction of each of the following boxes is shaded.

   a)

   _____ is shaded

   b)

   _____ is shaded

   c)

   _____ is shaded

   d)

   _____ is shaded

4. Using a **ruler**, complete the following figures to make a whole.

   a) $\frac{1}{2}$

   b) $\frac{1}{3}$

   c) $\frac{1}{4}$

5. Sketch a pie cut in …

   a) thirds

   b) quarters (or fourths)

   c) eighths

6. You have $\frac{3}{5}$ of a pie.

   a) What does the bottom (denominator) of the fraction tell you?

   b) What does the top (numerator) of the fraction tell you?

7. Explain why each picture does (or does not) show $\frac{1}{4}$.

   a)

   b)

   c)

   d)

Fractions can name parts of a set: $\frac{3}{5}$ of the figures are triangles, $\frac{1}{5}$ are squares and $\frac{1}{5}$ are circles.

1. Fill in the blanks.

a)

_____ of the figures are circles.

_____ of the figures are shaded.

b)

_____ of the figures are shaded.

_____ of the figures are triangles.

c)

_____ of the figures are triangles.

_____ of the figures are squares.

_____ of the figures are shaded.

_____ of the figures are unshaded.

2. Fill in the blanks.

$\frac{4}{8}$ of the figures are _____ .

$\frac{3}{8}$ of the figures are _____ .

$\frac{1}{8}$ of the figures are _____ .

3. Write 4 fraction statements for the picture:

a) _____ .

b) _____ .

c) _____ .

d) _____ .

4.

Can you describe this picture in two different ways using the fraction $\frac{3}{5}$?

_____

_____

5. A soccer team wins 5 games and loses 3 games.

a) How many games did the team play? _____

b) What <u>fraction</u> of the games did the team win? _____

6. A basketball team wins 7 games, loses 2 games and ties 3 games. What fractions of the games did the team …

a) win? _____   b) lose? _____   c) tie? _____

7. A box contains 4 blue markers, 3 black markers and 3 red markers.

What fraction of the markers are <u>not</u> blue? _____

8. Julie lives 3 km from her school.
She has biked 1 km towards her school.
What fraction of the distance to her school does she still have to bike?

9. Pia is 9 years old.
She lived in Calgary for 4 years, before she moved to Regina.
What fraction of her life did she live in Calgary?

10. Draw a picture to solve the puzzle.

a) There are 5 circles and squares.

$\frac{3}{5}$ of the figures are squares.

$\frac{2}{5}$ of the figures are shaded.

Two circles are shaded.

b) There are 5 triangles and squares.

$\frac{3}{5}$ of the figures are shaded.

$\frac{2}{5}$ of the figures are triangles.

One square is shaded.

NS4-73: Parts and Wholes

1. What fraction is shaded? How do you know?

2. 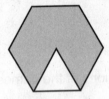 Draw lines from the point in the centre of the hexagon to the vertices of the hexagon.

   How many triangles cover the hexagon? _____

3. What fraction of each figure is the shaded part?

   a) 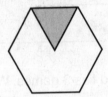   b) 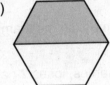   c) 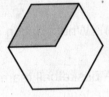   d)

   _____   _____   _____   _____

4. What fraction of the figure is the shaded piece?

   a)   b)   c)   d)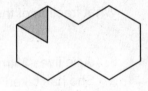

   _____   _____   _____   _____

TEACHER: Give your students pattern blocks or a copy of the pattern block blackline master from the Teacher's Guide.

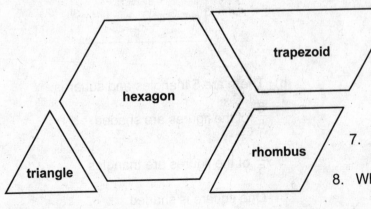

5. What fraction of the trapezoid is the triangle? (How many triangles will fit in the trapezoid?)

6. What fraction of the hexagon is the trapezoid?

7. What fraction of the hexagon is the rhombus?

8. What fraction of the hexagon is the triangle?

9. What fraction of two hexagons is the triangle?

Number Sense 2

1. 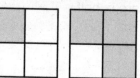 What fraction has a greater numerator, $\frac{1}{4}$ or $\frac{3}{4}$?

   Which fraction is greater?

   REMEMBER:
   $\frac{3}{4}$ ← numerator
   ← denominator

   Explain your thinking. _____

   _____

2. Circle the greater fraction in each pair.

   a) $\frac{3}{14}$ or $\frac{6}{14}$ b) $\frac{4}{12}$ or $\frac{7}{12}$ c) $\frac{2}{9}$ or $\frac{5}{9}$ d) $\frac{4}{7}$ or $\frac{5}{7}$

   e) $\frac{7}{27}$ or $\frac{4}{27}$ f) $\frac{13}{98}$ or $\frac{20}{98}$ g) $\frac{47}{125}$ or $\frac{46}{125}$ h) $\frac{88}{287}$ or $\frac{42}{287}$

3. Write the fractions in order from least to greatest.

   a) $\frac{2}{3}$, $\frac{1}{3}$, $\frac{3}{3}$ b) $\frac{2}{10}$, $\frac{1}{10}$, $\frac{7}{10}$, $\frac{9}{10}$ c) $\frac{5}{17}$, $\frac{9}{17}$, $\frac{8}{17}$, $\frac{16}{17}$

4. Write a fraction that is …

   a) greater than $\frac{3}{7}$ and less than $\frac{6}{7}$: _____

   b) greater than $\frac{1}{8}$ and less than $\frac{4}{8}$: _____

   c) greater than $\frac{3}{10}$ and less than $\frac{7}{10}$: _____

   d) greater than $\frac{8}{15}$ and less than $\frac{11}{15}$: _____

   e) greater than $\frac{14}{57}$ and less than $\frac{19}{57}$: _____

   f) greater than $\frac{58}{127}$ and less than $\frac{63}{127}$: _____

5. Two fractions have the same <u>denominators</u> (bottoms) but different <u>numerators</u> (tops). How can you tell which fraction is greater?

   _____

1.

   a) Trace and cut out this square. Then cut the square in half.

   What fraction of the square is each part?

   b) Next, cut each of these parts in half.

   What fraction of the square is each new part?

   c) As the denominator (bottom) of the fraction <u>increases</u>, what happens to the size of each piece?

   _____

2. Circle the <u>greatest</u> fraction in each pair.

   a) $\dfrac{1}{5}$ or $\dfrac{1}{7}$ b) $\dfrac{3}{15}$ or $\dfrac{3}{7}$ c) $\dfrac{2}{197}$ or $\dfrac{2}{297}$ d) $\dfrac{17}{52}$ or $\dfrac{17}{57}$

   e) $\dfrac{1}{3}$ or $\dfrac{1}{9}$ f) $\dfrac{7}{11}$ or $\dfrac{7}{13}$ g) $\dfrac{6}{15}$ or $\dfrac{6}{18}$ h) $\dfrac{3}{27}$ or $\dfrac{3}{42}$

3. Write the fractions in order from least to greatest.

   a) $\dfrac{1}{5}$, $\dfrac{1}{2}$, $\dfrac{1}{4}$ b) $\dfrac{1}{5}$, $\dfrac{1}{8}$, $\dfrac{1}{7}$ c) $\dfrac{2}{3}$, $\dfrac{2}{5}$, $\dfrac{2}{7}$

   _____   _____   _____

   BONUS

   d) $\dfrac{5}{7}$, $\dfrac{5}{5}$, $\dfrac{5}{11}$ e) $\dfrac{3}{11}$, $\dfrac{3}{4}$, $\dfrac{3}{8}$ f) $\dfrac{5}{8}$, $\dfrac{5}{11}$, $\dfrac{7}{8}$

   _____   _____   _____

4. Which fraction is greater, $\dfrac{1}{2}$ or $\dfrac{1}{100}$? ☐ Explain your thinking.

   _____

   _____

5. Fraction A and Fraction B have the same <u>numerators</u> (tops) but different <u>denominators</u> (bottoms). How can you tell which fraction is greater?

   _____

1. Using a ruler, divide each line into 2 equal parts.

   a) ———————————

   b) —————————————————————

   c) ——————————————————

   d) ———————————————————————————

2. Divide each line into 3 equal parts.

   a) ———————————————————

   b) ————————————————————————

   c) ——————————————————————————————

3. Draw the whole.

   a) $\frac{1}{2}$

   b) $\frac{1}{2}$

   c) $\frac{1}{3}$

4. Fill in the blanks.

   a) $\frac{1}{2}$ and ☐ make 1 whole

   b) $\frac{1}{3}$ and ☐ make 1 whole

   c) $\frac{1}{5}$ and ☐ make 1 whole

   d) $\frac{3}{7}$ and ☐ make 1 whole

5.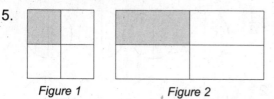

   Figure 1   Figure 2

   Is $\frac{1}{4}$ of Figure 1 the same size as $\frac{1}{4}$ of Figure 2?

   Explain why or why not.

6. Is it possible for $\frac{1}{4}$ of a pie to be bigger than $\frac{1}{3}$ of another pie? Show your thinking with a picture.

7. Ken ate $\frac{3}{5}$ of a pie. Karen ate the rest. Who ate more pie?
   Explain.

NS4-77: Mixed Fractions

Alan and his friends ate
the amount of pie shown:

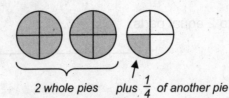

2 whole pies   plus $\frac{1}{4}$ of another pie

They ate two and one quarter pies altogether (or $2\frac{1}{4}$ pies). Note that $2\frac{1}{4}$ is called a **mixed fraction** because it is a mixture of a whole number and a fraction.

---

1. Write how many <u>whole</u> pies are shaded.

a) 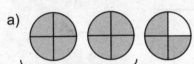   b) 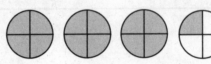   c)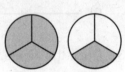

____2____ whole pies   _____ whole pies   _____ whole pie

2. Write the fractions as <u>mixed</u> fractions.

a) 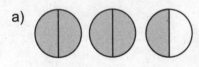   b) 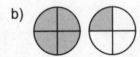   c)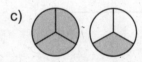

_____   _____   _____

d) 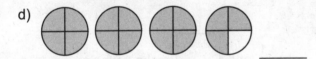   e)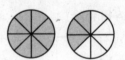

_____   _____

f) 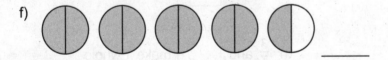   g)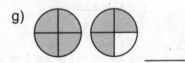

_____   _____

3. Shade the amount of pie given.
   NOTE: There may be more pies than you need.

a) $2\frac{1}{2}$    b) $3\frac{1}{2}$

c) $1\frac{1}{2}$    d) $2\frac{2}{3}$

e) $3\frac{3}{4}$ 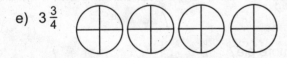   f) $1\frac{4}{5}$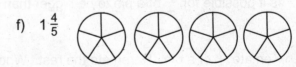

4. Sketch.   a) $2\frac{1}{2}$ pies   b) $3\frac{1}{2}$ pies   c) $2\frac{1}{4}$ pies   d) $3\frac{2}{3}$ pies

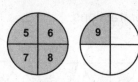

Improper Fraction: Mixed Fraction:

$$\frac{9}{4} \quad = \quad 2\frac{1}{4}$$

Alan and his friends ate **9** quarter-sized pieces of pizza. Altogether they ate $\frac{9}{4}$ pizzas.

Note that when the numerator of a fraction is larger than the denominator, the fraction represents <u>more than</u> a whole. Such fractions are called **improper fractions**.

----

1. Write these fractions as <u>improper</u> fractions.

a)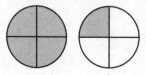

b)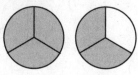

c)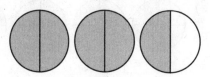

d)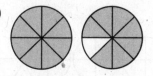

e)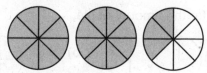

f)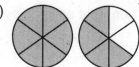

g)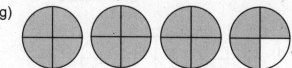

h)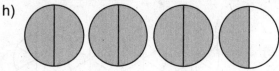

2. Shade one piece at a time until you have shaded the amount of pie given.

a) $\frac{5}{2}$

b) $\frac{7}{2}$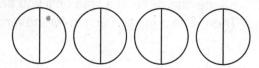

c) $\frac{8}{3}$

d) $\frac{13}{4}$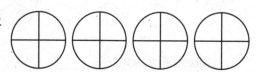

3. Sketch.　　a) $\frac{3}{2}$ pies　　b) $\frac{9}{2}$ pies　　c) $\frac{10}{4}$ pies　　d) $\frac{10}{3}$ pies

4. Which fractions are more than a whole?　　a) $\frac{3}{4}$　　b) $\frac{9}{4}$　　c) $\frac{7}{5}$

How do you know?

Number Sense 2

NS4-79: Mixed and Improper Fractions

1. Write these fractions as <u>mixed</u> fractions and as <u>improper</u> fractions.

a)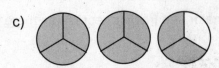

b)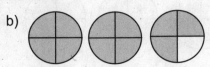

c)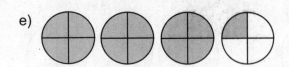

d)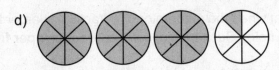

e)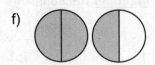

f)

2. Shade the amount of pie given.
   Then write an <u>improper</u> fraction for the amount of pie.

a) $2\frac{1}{2}$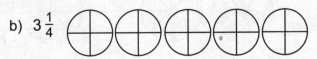

Improper Fraction: _____

b) $3\frac{1}{4}$

Improper Fraction: _____

c) $2\frac{1}{6}$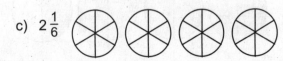

Improper Fraction: _____

d) $2\frac{5}{8}$

Improper Fraction: _____

3. Shade one piece at a time until you have shaded the amount of pie given.
   Then write a <u>mixed</u> fraction for the amount of pie.

a) $\frac{7}{3}$

Mixed Fraction: _____

b) $\frac{13}{6}$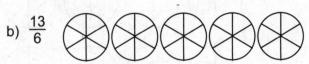

Mixed Fraction: _____

c) $\frac{7}{4}$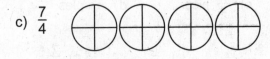

Mixed Fraction: _____

d) $\frac{12}{5}$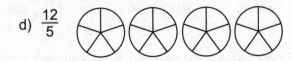

Mixed Fraction: _____

TEACHER:
Your students will need pattern blocks for this exercise, or a copy of the pattern blocks blackline master.

NOTE: The blocks shown here are not actual size!

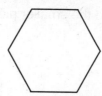

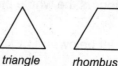

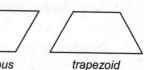

triangle   rhombus   trapezoid

hexagon

Euclid's Bakery sells hexagonal pies. They sell pieces shaped like triangles, rhombuses and trapezoids.

1. A hexagon represents a whole pie.

   a) Shade $2\frac{1}{6}$ pies.

   b) How many pieces did you shade? _____

   c) Write an improper fraction for the amount of pie shaded. _____

2. Make a model of the pies below with pattern blocks. (Place the smaller shapes on top of the hexagons.) Then write a mixed and improper fraction for each pie.

   a)

   Mixed Fraction: _____

   Improper Fraction: _____

   b)

   Mixed Fraction: _____

   Improper Fraction: _____

   c)

   Mixed Fraction: _____

   Improper Fraction: _____

3. Use the hexagon as the whole pie.
   Use the triangles, rhombuses, and trapezoids as the pieces.
   Make a pattern block model of the fractions below. Then sketch your models on the grid.

   a) $2\frac{1}{2}$    b) $1\frac{1}{2}$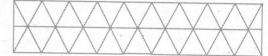

   c) $2\frac{1}{6}$ 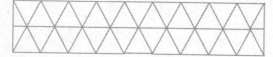   d) $1\frac{5}{6}$

   e) $1\frac{2}{3}$ 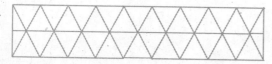   f) $3\frac{1}{3}$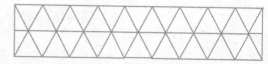

NS4-80: Investigating Mixed & Improper Fractions (continued)

4. Using the hexagon as the whole pie and the smaller pieces as parts, make a pattern block model of the fractions.

   Sketch your model below.

   a) $\frac{5}{2}$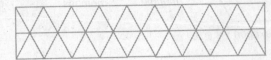

   b) $\frac{7}{6}$

   c) $\frac{7}{3}$

   d) $\frac{10}{3}$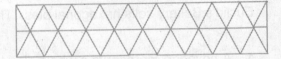

   e) $\frac{11}{6}$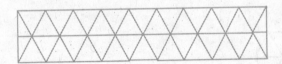

   f) $\frac{6}{2}$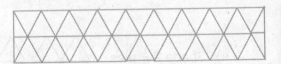

5. Using the trapezoid as the whole pie, and triangles as the pieces, make a pattern block model of the fractions. Sketch your models on the grid. The first one is done for you.

   a) $\frac{5}{3}$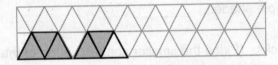

   b) $\frac{7}{3}$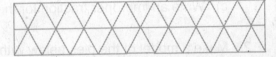

   c) $1\frac{2}{3}$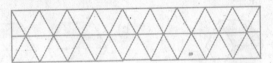

   d) $2\frac{1}{3}$

   e) $\frac{8}{3}$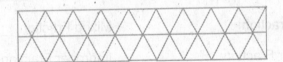

   f) $3\frac{2}{3}$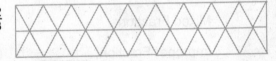

6. Draw sketches (using the hexagon as the whole) to find out which fraction is greater in each pair. Circle the greater fraction.

   a) $1\frac{5}{6}$ or $\frac{9}{6}$

   b) $2\frac{1}{6}$ or $\frac{14}{6}$

   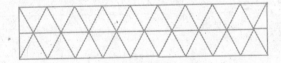
   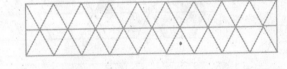

There are 4 quarter pieces in 1 pie.

There are 8 (2 × 4) quarters in 2 pies.

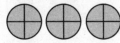

There are 12 (3 × 4) quarters in 3 pies.

How many quarter pieces are in $3\frac{3}{4}$ pies?

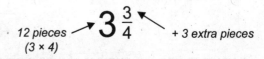

12 pieces (3 × 4) → $3\frac{3}{4}$ ← + 3 extra pieces

So there are 15 quarter pieces altogether.

----

1. Find the number of **halves** in each amount.

   a) 1 pie = _____ halves   b) 2 pies = _____ halves   c) 3 pies = _____ halves

   d) $1\frac{1}{2}$ pies = _____ halves   e) $2\frac{1}{2}$ pies = _____ halves   f) $3\frac{1}{2}$ pies = _____

2. Find the number of **thirds** in each amount.

   a) 1 pie = _____ thirds   b) 2 pies = _____ thirds   c) 3 pies = _____ thirds

   d) $1\frac{1}{3}$ pies = _____ thirds   e) $2\frac{2}{3}$ pies = _____   f) $3\frac{1}{3}$ pies = _____

3. Find the number of **quarters** (or fourths) in each amount.

   a) 1 pie = _____ quarters   b) 2 pies = _____ quarters   c) 3 pies = _____ quarters

   d) $2\frac{1}{4}$ pies = _____ quarters   e) $2\frac{3}{4}$ pies = _____   f) $3\frac{3}{4}$ pies = _____

4. A box holds 4 cans.

   a) 2 boxes hold _____ cans   b) $3\frac{1}{4}$ boxes hold _____ cans   c) $4\frac{3}{4}$ boxes hold _____ cans

5. A box holds 6 cans.

   a) $2\frac{1}{6}$ boxes hold _____ cans   b) $2\frac{5}{6}$ boxes hold _____ cans   c) $3\frac{1}{6}$ boxes hold _____ cans

6. Pens come in packs of 8. Dan used $1\frac{5}{8}$ packs. How many pens did he use? _____

7. Bottles come in packs of 6. How many bottles are in $2\frac{1}{2}$ packs? _____

NS4-82: Mixed and Improper Fractions (Advanced)

How many whole pies are there in $\frac{13}{4}$ pies?

There are 13 pieces altogether. ⟵ $\dfrac{13}{4}$ ⟶ *Each pie has 4 pieces.*

So you can find the number of whole pies by dividing 13 by 4:

13 ÷ 4 = 3 Remainder 1

There are 3 whole pies and 1 quarter left over. So $\frac{13}{4}$ = $3\frac{1}{4}$.

- -

1. Find the number of whole pies in each amount by dividing.

   a) $\frac{4}{2}$ pies = _____ whole pies   b) $\frac{6}{2}$ pies = _____ whole pies   c) $\frac{10}{2}$ pies = _____ whole pies

   d) $\frac{6}{3}$ pies = _____ whole pies   e) $\frac{12}{3}$ pies = _____ whole pies   f) $\frac{8}{4}$ pies = _____ whole pies

2. Find the number of whole pies and the number of pieces remaining by dividing.

   a) $\frac{5}{2}$ pies = ___2___ whole pies and ___1___ half pie = __$2\frac{1}{2}$__ pies

   b) $\frac{7}{2}$ pies = _____ whole pies and _____ half pies = _____ pies

   c) $\frac{7}{3}$ pies = _____ whole pies and _____ third pies = _____ pies

   d) $\frac{10}{3}$ pies = _____ whole pies and _____ third pies = _____ pies

   e) $\frac{11}{4}$ pies = _____ whole pies and _____ quarter pies = _____ pies

3. Write the following improper fractions as mixed fractions.

   a) $\frac{3}{2}$ =   b) $\frac{9}{2}$ =   c) $\frac{8}{3}$ =   d) $\frac{15}{4}$ =   e) $\frac{22}{5}$ =

4. Write a mixed and improper fraction for the number of litres.

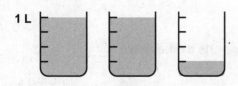

   Mixed _____   Improper _____

5. Write a mixed and improper fraction for the length of the rope.

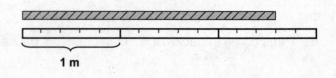

   Mixed _____   Improper _____

jump math
MULTIPLYING POTENTIAL

Number Sense 2

NS4-83: Equivalent Fractions

1. Circle the greater fraction. (If they are the same, circle "same.")

a) 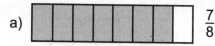 $\frac{7}{8}$ b) 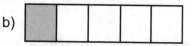 $\frac{1}{5}$ c)  $\frac{1}{3}$

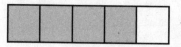 $\frac{4}{5}$ 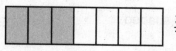 $\frac{3}{7}$ 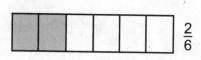 $\frac{2}{6}$

SAME   SAME   SAME

2. One third is equal to two sixths. One third and two sixths are **equivalent** fractions.
   Complete the equivalent fractions.

a) $\frac{1}{2} = \frac{}{4}$ b) $\frac{1}{2} = \frac{}{6}$

c) $\frac{1}{3} = \frac{}{6}$ d) $\frac{2}{3} = \frac{}{6}$

e) 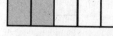 $\frac{3}{3} = \frac{}{10}$ f) $\frac{4}{10} = \frac{}{5}$

3. Use the picture to find the equivalent fractions.

1 whole							
$\frac{1}{2}$				$\frac{1}{2}$			
$\frac{1}{4}$		$\frac{1}{4}$		$\frac{1}{4}$		$\frac{1}{4}$	
$\frac{1}{8}$	$\frac{1}{8}$	$\frac{1}{8}$	$\frac{1}{8}$	$\frac{1}{8}$	$\frac{1}{8}$	$\frac{1}{8}$	$\frac{1}{8}$

a) $\frac{1}{4} = \frac{}{8}$ b) $\frac{1}{2} = \frac{}{8}$

c) $\frac{6}{8} = \frac{}{4}$ d) $\frac{2}{4} = \frac{}{2}$

4. Use the picture to find the equivalent fractions.

1 whole									
$\frac{1}{5}$		$\frac{1}{5}$		$\frac{1}{5}$		$\frac{1}{5}$		$\frac{1}{5}$	
$\frac{1}{10}$	$\frac{1}{10}$	$\frac{1}{10}$	$\frac{1}{10}$	$\frac{1}{10}$	$\frac{1}{10}$	$\frac{1}{10}$	$\frac{1}{10}$	$\frac{1}{10}$	$\frac{1}{10}$

a) $\frac{1}{5} = \frac{}{10}$ b) $\frac{6}{10} = \frac{}{5}$

c) $\frac{4}{5} = \frac{}{10}$ d) $\frac{5}{5} = \frac{}{10}$

Number Sense 2

NS4-84: More Equivalent Fractions

George shades $\frac{4}{6}$ of the squares in an array.

He then draws heavy lines around the squares to group them into 3 equal groups.

He sees that $\frac{2}{3}$ of the squares are shaded.

Four sixths are equal to two thirds: $\frac{4}{6} = \frac{2}{3}$. Four sixths and two thirds are equivalent fractions.

---

1. Group the squares (by drawing heavy lines) to show …

    a) Two eighths equals one fourth ($\frac{2}{8} = \frac{1}{4}$).

    b) Four eighths equals one half ($\frac{4}{8} = \frac{1}{2}$).

    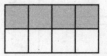

2. Group the squares to show an equivalent fraction.

    a)

    $\frac{3}{6} = \frac{}{2}$

    b)
    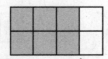

    $\frac{6}{8} = \frac{}{4}$

    c)

    $\frac{6}{9} = \frac{}{3}$

    d)
    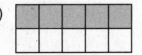

    $\frac{5}{10} = \frac{1}{}$

    e)

    $\frac{2}{6} = \frac{1}{}$

    f)
    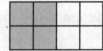

    $\frac{4}{8} = \frac{1}{}$

    g)

    $\frac{6}{9} = \frac{}{}$

    h)
    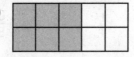

    $\frac{6}{10} = \frac{}{}$

    i)
    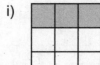

    $\frac{3}{9} = \frac{}{}$

3. Shade squares to make an equivalent fraction.

    a)

    $\frac{1}{2} = \frac{}{12}$

    b)

    $\frac{1}{3} = \frac{}{12}$

    c)
    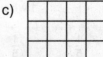

    $\frac{1}{4} = \frac{}{12}$

Number Sense 2

NS4-85: Further Equivalent Fractions

1. Group the buttons to make an equivalent fraction.

   a)

   $\frac{2}{6} = \frac{1}{3}$

   b) ○○○○

   $\frac{2}{4} = \frac{}{2}$

   c) ○○○○○○

   $\frac{3}{6} = \frac{}{2}$

   d)

   $\frac{6}{9} = \frac{}{3}$

   e)

   $\frac{8}{10} = \frac{}{5}$

   f) ○○○○○○○○○

   $\frac{3}{9} = \frac{}{}$

   g) ○○○○○○○○○○

   $\frac{2}{10} = \frac{}{}$

2. Group the pieces to make an equivalent fraction.
   The grouping in the first question has already been done for you.

   a) 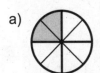 $\frac{2}{8} = \frac{}{4}$

   b)  $\frac{2}{6} = \frac{}{3}$

   c)  $\frac{2}{10} = \frac{}{5}$

   d) 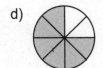 $\frac{6}{8} = \frac{}{}$

   e) 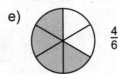 $\frac{4}{6} = \frac{}{}$

   f)  $\frac{4}{10} = \frac{}{}$

3. Cut each pie into smaller pieces to make an equivalent fraction.

   a) $\frac{2}{3} = \frac{}{6}$

   b) $\frac{2}{3} = \frac{}{9}$

   c)  $\frac{1}{2} = \frac{}{4}$

4. Write two different fractions for each shaded set.

   a) ⊡⊡⊡ □□□   b) ⬠⬠ ⬠⬠ ⬠⬠ ⬠⬠   c) △△△ △△△ △△△

   d) △△ △△ △△ △△   e) ●●●● ○○○○   f) ⬠⬠⬠⬠ ⬠⬠⬠⬠

5. Draw shaded and unshaded circles (as in Question 1) and group the circles to show.

   a) six eighths is equivalent to three quarters

   b) four fifths is equivalent to eight tenths

6. Dan says that $\frac{1}{2}$ is equivalent to $\frac{2}{4}$. Is he right? How do you know?

NS4-86: Sharing and Fractions

Dan has 6 cookies.

He wants to give $\frac{2}{3}$ of his cookies to his friends.
To do so, he shares the cookies equally onto 3 plates.

There are 3 equal groups, so each group is $\frac{1}{3}$ of 6.

There are 2 cookies in each group, so $\frac{1}{3}$ of 6 is 2.

There are 4 cookies in two groups, so $\frac{2}{3}$ of 6 is 4.

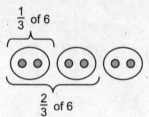

----

1. Write a fraction for the amount of dots shown. The first one has been done for you.

a)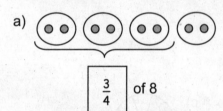

$\frac{3}{4}$ of 8

b)

☐ of 15

c)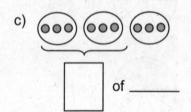

☐ of _____

d)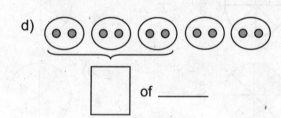

☐ of _____

2. Fill in the missing numbers.

a) $\frac{1}{3}$ of 6 = _____

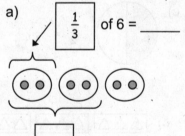

☐ of _____ = _____

b) ☐ of 8 = _____

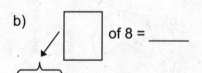

☐ of _____ = _____

c) ☐ of 9 = _____

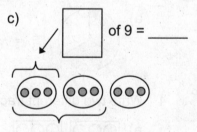

☐ of _____ = _____

d)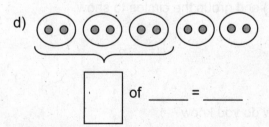

☐ of _____ = _____

e)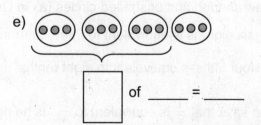

☐ of _____ = _____

NS4-86: Sharing and Fractions (continued)

3. Draw a circle to show the given amount. The first one has been done for you.

a) $\frac{2}{3}$ of 6

b) $\frac{3}{4}$ of 8

c) $\frac{3}{5}$ of 10

d) $\frac{3}{4}$ of 12

e) $\frac{4}{5}$ of 10

f) $\frac{2}{3}$ of 9

4. Fill in the correct number of dots in each circle, then draw a larger circle to show the given amount.

a) $\frac{2}{3}$ of 12

b) $\frac{2}{3}$ of 9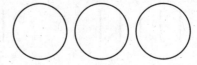

c) $\frac{1}{2}$ of 8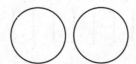

d) $\frac{3}{4}$ of 8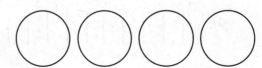

5. Find the fraction of the whole amount by sharing the cookies equally.

   HINT: Draw the correct number of plates then place the cookies one at a time. Then circle the correct amount.

a) Find $\frac{1}{4}$ of 8 cookies.

b) Find $\frac{1}{2}$ of 10 cookies.

$\frac{1}{4}$ of 8 is _____

$\frac{1}{2}$ of 10 is _____

c) Find $\frac{2}{3}$ of 6 cookies.

d) Find $\frac{3}{4}$ of 12 cookies.

$\frac{2}{3}$ of 6 is _____

$\frac{3}{4}$ of 12 is _____

e) Find $\frac{1}{2}$ of 12 cookies.

f) Find $\frac{3}{5}$ of 10 cookies.

$\frac{1}{2}$ of 12 is _____

$\frac{3}{5}$ of 10 is _____

1. Gerome finds $\frac{1}{3}$ of 6 by dividing: 6 divided into 3 groups gives 2 in each group ($6 \div 3 = 2$).

   Find the fraction of each of the following numbers by writing an equivalent division statement.

   a) $\frac{1}{2}$ of 8 = 4   b) $\frac{1}{2}$ of 10   c) $\frac{1}{2}$ of 16   d) $\frac{1}{2}$ of 20

   ___8 ÷ 2 = 4___   _____   _____   _____

   e) $\frac{1}{3}$ of 9   f) $\frac{1}{3}$ of 15   g) $\frac{1}{4}$ of 12   h) $\frac{1}{6}$ of 18

   _____   _____   _____   _____

2. Circle $\frac{1}{2}$ of each set of lines.

   HINT: Count the lines and divide by 2.

   a) | | | | | b) | | | | | | | | c) | | | |

   d) | | | | | | | | | | | e) | | | | | | | | | | | | |

3. Shade $\frac{1}{3}$ of each set of circles. Then circle $\frac{2}{3}$. The first one is done for you.

   a)    b)

   c) ○ ○ ○   d)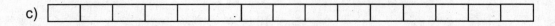

4. Circle $\frac{1}{4}$ of each set of triangles.

   a) △ △ △ △   b) △ △ △ △ △ △ △ △ △ △

   c) △ △ △ △ △ △ △ △ △ △ △ △ △ △ △ △

5. Shade $\frac{3}{5}$ of the boxes.

   HINT: First count the boxes and find $\frac{1}{5}$.

   a) [grid of boxes]   b) [grid of boxes]

   c) [grid of boxes]

1. Sarah has 8 pennies.

   She loses 2.

   To find out what fraction of her pennies she lost, she draws 8 dots (in groups of 2).

   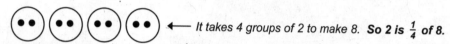 ← *It takes 4 groups of 2 to make 8.* **So 2 is $\frac{1}{4}$ of 8.**

   Sarah lost $\frac{1}{4}$ of her pennies.

   Complete each statement by first drawing a picture. The first one has been done for you.

   a) 2 is $\boxed{\dfrac{1}{3}}$ of 6   b) 2 is $\boxed{}$ of 4   c) 3 is $\boxed{}$ of 12

   d) 3 is $\boxed{}$ of 9   e) 4 is $\boxed{}$ of 12   f) 5 is $\boxed{}$ of 15

2. A soccer team plays 12 games. They win 5 games.
   Did they win more than half their games?
   Explain how you know.

3. Andy finds $\frac{2}{3}$ of 12 as follows:

   - First he divides 12 by 3.
   - Then he multiplies the result by 2.

   Draw a picture using dots and circles to show why this would work.

   Then find $\frac{2}{3}$ of 15 using Andy's method.

4. Gerald has 10 oranges. He gives away $\frac{3}{5}$ of the oranges.

   a) How many did he give away?

   b) How many did he keep?

   c) How did you find your answer to part b)? (Did you use a calculation, a picture, a model or a list?)

1. Fill in the missing mixed fractions on the number line.

a)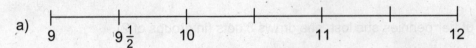
9   9 $\frac{1}{2}$ 10   11   12

b)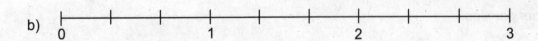
0   1   2   3

c)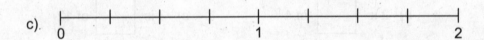
0   1   2

d)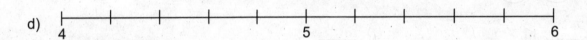
4   5   6

e)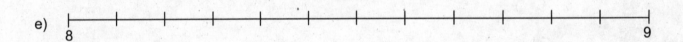
8   9

2. Continue the patterns.

a) $3\frac{2}{5}$, $3\frac{3}{5}$, $3\frac{4}{5}$, _____ , _____   b) $4\frac{3}{7}$, $4\frac{4}{7}$, $4\frac{5}{7}$, _____ , _____

3. Fill in the blanks.

a) $2\frac{1}{4}$ pies = __9__ quarters   b) $3\frac{3}{4}$ pies = _____ quarters   c) $4\frac{1}{4}$ pies = _____ quarters

$2\frac{1}{4}$ = $\frac{9}{4}$ $3\frac{3}{4}$ = $4\frac{1}{4}$ =

d) $3\frac{1}{3}$ pies = _____ thirds   e) $4\frac{2}{3}$ pies = _____ thirds   f) $5\frac{1}{3}$ pies = _____ thirds

$3\frac{1}{3}$ = $4\frac{2}{3}$ = $5\frac{1}{3}$ =

g) $2\frac{2}{5}$ pies = _____ fifths   h) $1\frac{4}{5}$ pies = _____ fifths   i) $3\frac{2}{5}$ pies = _____ fifths

$2\frac{2}{5}$ = $1\frac{4}{5}$ = $3\frac{2}{5}$ =

1. Imagine moving the shaded pieces from pies A and B into pie plate C. Show how much of pie C would be filled then write a fraction for pie C.

A   B   C

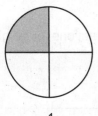 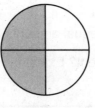 

$$\frac{1}{4} \qquad + \qquad \frac{2}{4} \qquad = \qquad \underline{\quad}$$

2. Imagine pouring the liquid from cups A and B into cup C.
   Shade the amount of liquid that would be in C.
   Then complete the addition statements.

   a) 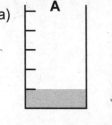   b)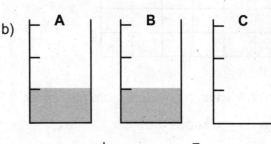

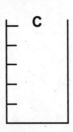

$$\underline{\quad} \atop 5 \quad + \quad {\underline{\quad} \atop 5} \quad = \quad \underline{\quad} \qquad\qquad {\underline{\quad} \atop 3} \quad + \quad {\underline{\quad} \atop 3} \quad = \quad \underline{\quad}$$

3. Add.

   a) $\frac{3}{5} + \frac{1}{5} =$ b) $\frac{2}{4} + \frac{1}{4} =$ c) $\frac{3}{7} + \frac{2}{7} =$ d) $\frac{5}{8} + \frac{2}{8} =$

   e) $\frac{3}{11} + \frac{7}{11} =$ f) $\frac{5}{17} + \frac{9}{17} =$ g) $\frac{11}{24} + \frac{10}{24} =$ h) $\frac{18}{57} + \frac{13}{57} =$

4. Show how much pie would be left if you took away the amount shown.
   Then complete the fraction statement.

   a) 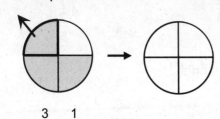   b)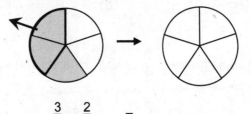

$$\frac{3}{4} - \frac{1}{4} \quad = \quad \underline{\quad} \qquad\qquad\qquad \frac{3}{5} - \frac{2}{5} \quad = \quad \underline{\quad}$$

5. Subtract.

   a) $\frac{2}{3} - \frac{1}{3} =$ b) $\frac{3}{5} - \frac{2}{5} =$ c) $\frac{6}{7} - \frac{3}{7} =$ d) $\frac{5}{8} - \frac{2}{8} =$

   e) $\frac{9}{12} - \frac{2}{12} =$ f) $\frac{6}{19} - \frac{4}{19} =$ g) $\frac{9}{28} - \frac{3}{28} =$ h) $\frac{17}{57} - \frac{12}{57} =$

1.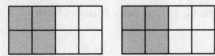

   Show two different ways to group the squares into equal amounts. Are the fractions four eighths ($\frac{4}{8}$)

   two fourths ($\frac{2}{4}$) and one half ($\frac{1}{2}$) the same or different? Explain.

   _____

   _____

2.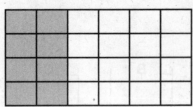

   Write four equivalent fractions for the amount shaded here.

   _____   _____   _____   _____

3. Which fraction represents more pie? $\frac{5}{2}$ or $\frac{7}{2}$?

   How do you know?

   _____

   _____

4. Draw a picture to find out which fraction is greater.

   a) $3\frac{1}{2}$ or $2\frac{1}{2}$ b) $\frac{7}{4}$ or $\frac{5}{4}$ c) $3\frac{1}{2}$ or $\frac{5}{2}$ d) $2\frac{1}{3}$ or $\frac{8}{3}$

5. Write the following mixed fractions as improper fractions.

   a) $2\frac{1}{4}$ b) $3\frac{2}{3}$ c) $2\frac{3}{5}$ d) $4\frac{1}{2}$

6. Which is greater: $\frac{7}{3}$ or $\frac{5}{2}$? How do you know? Draw a model.

7. Which two whole numbers is $\frac{7}{4}$ between?

8.

   Beth is making a black and white patchwork. Two thirds of the quilt has been completed (see diagram on left).

   How many black squares will be in the finished quilt?

NS4-92: Dollar and Cent Notation

The charts show how to represent money in cent notation and in dollar notation.

	Cent Notation	Dollar (Decimal) Notation		Cent Notation	Dollar (Decimal) Notation
Sixty-five cents	65¢	$0.65 dimes pennies	Seven cents	7¢	$0.07 dimes pennies

A dime is a <u>tenth</u> of a dollar. A penny is a <u>hundredth</u> of a dollar.

1. Write the total amount of money in cent and in dollar (decimal) notation.

a)

dimes	pennies
3	4

= __34__ ¢ = $ __0.34__

b)

dimes	pennies
0	5

= _____ ¢ = $ _____

c)

dimes	pennies
4	3

= _____ ¢ = $ _____

d)

dimes	pennies
8	7

= _____ ¢ = $ _____

e)

dimes	pennies
5	4

= _____ ¢ = $ _____

f)

dimes	pennies
0	9

= _____ ¢ = $ _____

g)

dimes	pennies
0	2

= _____ ¢ = $ _____

h)

dimes	pennies
7	5

= _____ ¢ = $ _____

i)

dimes	pennies
0	1

= _____ ¢ = $ _____

2. Count the given coins and write the total amount in cents and in dollar (decimal) notation.

a) 10¢ 10¢ 5¢ 5¢ 1¢ 1¢ 1¢

Total amount = _____ ¢ = $ _____

b) 25¢ 10¢ 10¢ 1¢ 1¢

Total amount = _____ ¢ = $ _____

c) 25¢ 25¢ 10¢ 10¢ 5¢ 1¢

Total amount = _____ ¢ = $ _____

d) 25¢ 25¢ 25¢ 10¢

Total amount = _____ ¢ = $ _____

e) 25¢ 10¢ 10¢ 10¢ 10¢ 5¢ 1¢

Total amount = _____ ¢ = $ _____

f) 25¢ 10¢ 10¢ 5¢ 5¢ 1¢ 1¢

Total amount = _____ ¢ = $ _____

BONUS

g) 25¢ 25¢ 10¢ 10¢ 10¢ 5¢ 1¢ 1¢ 1¢

Total amount = _____ ¢ = $ _____

jump math
MULTIPLYING POTENTIAL

Number Sense 2

3. Complete the chart.

	Amount in ¢	Dollars	Dimes	Pennies	Amount in $
a)	143¢	1	4	3	$ 1.43
b)	47¢				
c)	325¢				
d)	3¢				
e)	816¢				

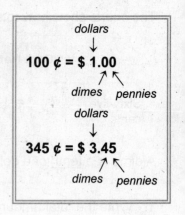

```
        dollars
           ↓
100 ¢ = $ 1.00
         ↗  ↖
     dimes  pennies

        dollars
           ↓
345 ¢ = $ 3.45
         ↗  ↖
     dimes  pennies
```

4. Write each amount in cent notation.

   a) $3.00 = ___300¢___   b) $0.60 = _____   c) $0.08 = _____   d) $1.00 = _____

   e) $7.00 = _____   f) $12.00 = _____   g) $15.00 = _____   h) $14.00 = _____

   i) $1.99 = _____   j) $1.11 = _____   k) $1.51 = _____   l) $1.37 = _____

   m) $0.98 = _____   n) $0.55 = _____   o) $0.03 = _____   p) $0.08 = _____

5. Write each amount in dollar notation.

   a) 254¢ = ___$2.54___   b) 103¢ = _____   c) 216¢ = _____   d) 375¢ = _____

   e) 300¢ = _____   f) 4¢ = _____   g) 7¢ = _____   h) 90¢ = _____

   i) 600¢ = _____   j) 1000¢ = _____   k) 1200¢ = _____   l) 1600¢ = _____

   m) 64¢ = _____   n) 99¢ = _____   o) 3¢ = _____   p) 56¢ = _____

6. Complete each pattern by counting by the type of coin pictured. Write your answers in cent notation and in dollar notation.

   a)
          b)

   25¢ , _____ , _____ , _____ , _____
            200¢ , _____ , _____ , _____ , _____

   $ .25 , _____ , _____ , _____ , _____
            $2.00 , _____ , _____ , _____ , _____

   c)
          d)

   _____ , _____ , _____
            _____ , _____ , _____ , _____

   _____ , _____ , _____
            _____ , _____ , _____ , _____

1. Complete the chart as shown in a).

Dollar Amount		Cent Amount		Total
a) ($2) ($1) = __$3__		(25¢) (10¢) = __35¢__		__$3.35__
b) ($2) ($2) ($2) = _____		(5¢) (5¢) (1¢) = _____		_____
c) ($2) ($2) = _____		(10¢) (10¢) (5¢) = _____		_____
d) ($2) ($2) ($2) = _____		(25¢) (25¢) (5¢) = _____		_____
e) [5] [5] = _____		(5¢) (1¢) (1¢) = _____		_____
f) [10] [10] = _____		(5¢) (5¢) (1¢) = _____		_____

2. Count the given coins. Write the total amount in cents and in dollars (decimals).

Coins	Cent Notation	Dollar Notation
a) (25¢) (25¢) (25¢) (25¢) (5¢)	__105¢__	__$1.05__
b) (25¢) (25¢) (25¢) (10¢) (10¢) (1¢)	_____	_____
c) (25¢) (25¢) (25¢) (25¢) (25¢) (25¢)	_____	_____
d) (25¢) (25¢) (25¢) (10¢) (10¢) (10¢) (5¢)	_____	_____

3. Alicia paid for a pencil with 3 coins. The pencil cost $ .75. Which coins did she use?

4. Alan bought a pack of markers for $3.50. He paid for it with 4 coins. Which coins did he use?

5. Tanya's daily allowance is $5.25. Her mom gave her 4 coins. Which coins did she use?

NS4-94: More Dollar and Cent Notation

Dollar notation and **cent notation** are related in the following way:

$1.00 = 100¢ $0.50 = 50¢ $0.05 = 5¢ $3.82 = 382¢

----

1. Change the amount in dollar notation to cent notation. Then circle the greater amount.

   a) 175¢   or $1.73   b) $1.00   or   101¢   c) 6¢   or $0.04

   d) $5.98   or   597¢   e) 650¢   or $6.05   f) $0.87   or   187¢

2. Write each amount in dollar notation. Then circle the greater amount of money in each pair.

   a) three dollars and eighty-five cents   or   three dollars and twenty-eight cents

   _____   _____

   b) nine dollars and seventy cents   or   nine dollars and eighty-two cents

   _____   _____

   c) eight dollars and seventy-five cents   or   863¢

   _____   _____

   d) twelve dollars and sixty cents   or $12.06

   _____   _____

3. Write each amount in cent notation then in dollar notation. The first question is done for you.

   a) 7 pennies   = __7¢__ = __$ .07__   b) 4 nickels   = _____ = _____   c) 6 dimes   = _____ = _____

   d) 4 pennies   = _____ = _____   e) 13 pennies   = _____ = _____   f) 1 quarter = _____ = _____

   g) 5 nickels   = _____ = _____   h) 3 quarters   = _____ = _____   i) 8 dimes   = _____ = _____

   j) 6 toonies   = _____ = _____   k) 4 loonies   = _____ = _____   l) 7 loonies   = _____ = _____

4. Which is a greater amount of money: 168¢ or $1.65? Explain. _____

   _____

jump math
MULTIPLYING POTENTIAL.

Jenny makes a chart with the **names** of the Canadian coins and the amount each is **worth**:

Penny	Nickel	Dime	Quarter	Loonie	Toonie
1 cent	5 cents	10 cents	25 cents	100 cents	200 cents
$0.01	$0.05	$0.10	$0.25	$1.00	$2.00
1¢	5¢	10¢	25¢	100¢	200¢

- -

1. Circle all the <u>correct</u> forms of writing amounts of (Canadian) money. Cross out the <u>incorrect</u> forms.

   Example: ($1.00) ~~$4.56832~~

   0.45¢   2.34$ $15.958 $10.05   &18.66   &56¢

   ¢23   ¢676 $85.32 $0.95   ¢36 $0.17

   ¢15.18 $25.30   36¢ $18.50 $95.99 $12.3560

2. Match the picture of each coin to its correct value.
   BE CAREFUL: There are more answers than coins.

   $3.00 $2.00 $1.00   25¢   1¢   10¢ $0.05   13¢ $0.75   15¢

3. Match the picture of each bill to its correct value. Again, there are more answers than bills.

   $5.00 $20.00 $100.00 $10.00 $50.00 $1000.00 $500.00

jump math
MULTIPLYING POTENTIAL

1. Add.

a)		5	3
+		4	2

b)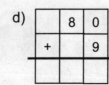

c)

d)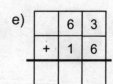

e)

2. Shelly spent $12.50 on a blouse and $4.35 on a pair of socks.

   To find out how much she spent, she added the amounts using the following steps:

	$	1	2 .	5	0
+	$		4 .	3	5

Step 1:
She lined up the decimal points and the numerals.

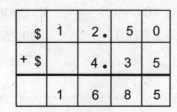

Step 2:
She added the numerals, starting with the pennies.

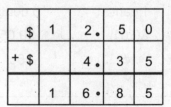

Step 3:
She added a decimal point to show the amount in dollars.

Find the total by adding.

a) $5.45 + $3.23

	$	5 .	4	5
+	$	3 .	2	3
		.		

b) $22.26 + $15.23

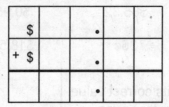

c) $18.16 + $20.32

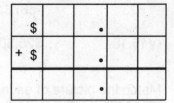

3. To add the amounts below, you will have to regroup.

a)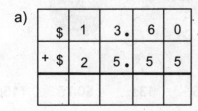

	$	1	3 .	6	0
+	$	2	5 .	5	5

b)

	$	1	8 .	2	5
+	$	5	3 .	1	2

c)

	$	4	5 .	2	0
+	$		6 .	5	5

d)

	$	3	2 .	6	0
+	$	2	8 .	0	0

e)

	$	1	5 .	6	0
+	$	1	9 .	2	5

f)

	$	2	9 .	1	0
+	$	1	9 .	6	5

Answer the following questions in your notebook.

4. Ari paid 23¢ for a muffin and 35¢ for an apple. How much did he spend in total?

5. Alan bought a book for $14.25 and a box of candles for $10.14. How much did he spend in total?

6. From her babysitting job, Meera saved 6 toonies, 5 dimes and 3 pennies.

    Kyle saved a 5 dollar bill, 3 toonies, 2.dimes and 4 pennies from his.

    Who saved more money?

7. Mansa has $18.

    a) If she spends $12.00 on a movie, can she buy a magazine for $3.29?

    b) If she buys a book for $7.50 and a cap for $9.00, can she buy a subway ticket for $2.25?

8. Four children bought dogs at an animal shelter.

    ✓ Anthony paid for his dog with 2 twenty dollar bills, 1 toonie, 1 loonie, 2 quarters and 1 nickel.

    ✓ Mike paid with 2 ten dollar bills, 8 toonies and 1 quarter.

    ✓ Sandor paid with 1 twenty and 1 ten dollar bill, 1 loonie and 3 quarters.

    ✓ Tory paid with 2 twenty dollar bills, 4 toonies, 1 loonie and 3 dimes.

    Find the amount each child paid. Then match their names with the dog they bought.

| Dog A | Dog B | Dog C | Dog D | Dog E | Dog F |
| $ 31.75 | $ 49.30 | $42.68 | $ 44.34 | $ 36.25 | $ 43.55 |

9. Try to find the answer mentally.

    a) How much do 3 roses cost at $1.25 each?

    b) How many lemons costing 30¢ could you buy with $1.00?

    c) Sketch pads cost $5.25. How many could you buy if you had $26.00?

1. Find the remaining amount by subtracting.

a)

$	2	.	8	4
− $	1	.	3	1

b)

$	7	.	2	9
− $	4	.	0	5

c)

$	9	.	6	7
− $	4	.	2	6

d)

$	7	.	8	6
− $	5	.	2	3

e)

$	5	.	5	4
− $	3	.	3	4

2. Subtract the given money amounts by regrouping once or twice.

Example:

Step 1:

		5	10	
$	~~6~~	.	~~0~~	0
− $	4	.	3	5
		.		

Step 2:

		5	9 ~~10~~	10
$	~~6~~	.	~~0~~	~~0~~
− $	4	.	3	5
$	1	.	6	5

a)

$	7	.	0	0
− $	4	.	4	5

b)

$	9	.	0	0
− $	3	.	2	6

c)

$	9	.	0	4
− $	8	.	9	5

d)

$	5	3	.	0	0
− $	2	2	.	3	1

e)

$	4	7	.	4	5
− $	3	8	.	4	5

f)

$	2	7	.	4	8
− $	1	3	.	6	6

3. Val has $1.85. He lends $1.45 to his friend.
   How much money does he have left?

4. Chris spent $4.23 on his lunch.
   He paid with a five dollar bill. Calculate his change.

5. Anya went to a grocery store with $10.00.
   Can she buy bread for $2.50, juice for $4.00 and cereal for $4.50?
   If not, by how much is she short?

6. Mark has $25.00.
   He wants to buy a shirt for $14.95 and pants for $16.80.
   How much extra money does he need to buy the pants and shirt?

NS4-98: Estimating

1. For each collection of coins and bills, estimate the amount to the nearest dollar and then count the precise amount.

	Estimate Total (to the nearest dollar)	Actual Total
a) 10 5 25¢ 5¢ 5¢ 1¢		
b) 20 10 25¢ 25¢ 25¢ 10¢		
c) 20 5 $2 10¢ 10¢ 1¢		
d) 10 10 $2 25¢ 25¢		

2. Round the given cent amounts to the nearest tens place. The first one has been done for you.

   a) 54¢ [50¢]   b) 35¢ [ ]

   c) 82¢ [ ]   d) 66¢ [ ]

   e) 45¢ [ ]   f) 71¢ [ ]

   g) 19¢ [ ]   h) 18¢ [ ]   i) 89¢ [ ]

   j) 14¢ [ ]   k) 38¢ [ ]   l) 56¢ [ ]

   REMEMBER:

   If the number in the <u>ones</u> digit is:

   0, 1, 2, 3 or 4 – you round **down**

   5, 6, 7, 8 or 9 – you round **up**

3. Circle the amount where the <u>cent</u> amount is less than 50¢. The first one has been done for you.

   a) ($8.45)   b) $6.80   c) $2.24   d) $8.74   e) $9.29   f) $5.55

   45 is less than 50

   g) $4.45   h) $3.50   i) $5.40   j) $9.29   k) $5.49   l) $7.51

4. Round the given amounts to the nearest dollar amount.

   a) $5.65 [$6.00]   b) $13.32 [ ]

   c) $22.75 [ ]   d) $6.55 [ ]

   e) $37.35 [ ]   f) $12.22 [ ]

   g) $48.15 [ ]   h) $411.50 [ ]   i) $4.24 [ ]

   j) $35.42 [ ]   k) $29.75 [ ]   l) $45.89 [ ]

   REMEMBER:

   If the cent amount is <u>less</u> than 50¢, you round **down**.

   If the cent amount is <u>equal to or more</u> than 50¢, you round **up**.

5. Estimate the following sums and differences by rounding each amount to the nearest dollar.

a)
$$\begin{array}{r} \$5.49 \\ + \$3.20 \end{array}$$

b)
$$\begin{array}{r} \$9.53 \\ - \$2.14 \end{array}$$

c)
$$\begin{array}{r} \$2.75 \\ + \$5.64 \end{array}$$

d)
$$\begin{array}{r} \$7.78 \\ - \$2.85 \end{array}$$

	$	5 .	0	0
+	$	3 .	0	0
	$	8 .	0	0

e)
$$\begin{array}{r} \$39.78 \\ - \$23.56 \end{array}$$

f)
$$\begin{array}{r} \$26.78 \\ + \$13.45 \end{array}$$

g)
$$\begin{array}{r} \$26.65 \\ + \$15.33 \end{array}$$

Solve the following word problems by rounding and estimating.

6. Jasmine has $10.00.
She bought a paintbrush for $2.27.
Estimate her change.

7. Tony spent $12.35 and Sayaka spent
$26.91 at the grocery store.
About how much more did Sayaka spend
than Tony?

8. Todd spent $8.64 on pop,
$6.95 on vegetables and dip,
and $12.64 on bagels.
About how much did
he spend altogether?

9. Donna bought school
supplies for her three children.
Each child's supplies
cost $13.78.
About how much money did
Donna spend?

10. For each problem below, make an estimate
and then find the exact amount.

a) Dianna has $4.26. Erick has $2.34.
How much more money does
Dianna have?

b) Maribel has $19.64. Sharon has $7.42.
How much money do they have altogether?

11. Jason has saved $16.95.
Does he have enough money to buy a
book for $8.77 and a binder for $6.93?

12. Explain why rounding to the nearest dollar isn't helpful for the following question:

"Patrick has $7.23. Jill has $6.92. About how much more money does Patrick have than Jill?"

NS4-99: Decimal Tenths

A **tenth** (or $\frac{1}{10}$) can be represented in different ways.

A tenth of a pie.

A tenth of the distance between 0 and 1.

A tenth of a hundreds block.

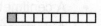
A tenth of a tens block.

Tenths commonly appear in units of measurement ("a millimetre is a tenth of a centimetre").

Mathematicians invented the decimal as a short form for tenths: $\frac{1}{10}$ = .1 (or 0.1), $\frac{2}{10}$ = .2 and so on.

- -

1. Write a fraction for each shaded part in the boxes below.

   a) 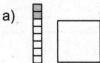   b)   c)   d)

2. Write a fraction AND a decimal for each shaded part in the boxes below.

   a) 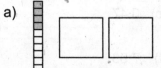   b) 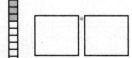   c) 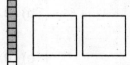   d)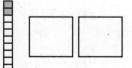

3. Write a decimal for each shaded part. Then add them together and shade your answer. The first one has been done for you.

   a) 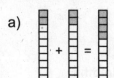 .2 + .2 = .4   b)   c)

   d) 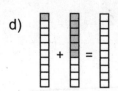   e) 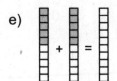   f)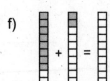

   g) 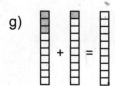   h) 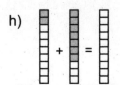   i)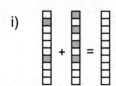

4. Continue the pattern: 0.2 , 0.4 , 0.6 , _____ , _____

Number Sense 2

NS4-100: Place Value (Decimals)

Fractions with denominators that are multiples of ten (tenths, hundredths) commonly appear in units of measurement.

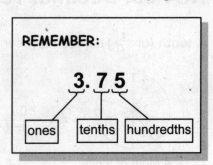

REMEMBER:

3. 7 5

ones | tenths | hundredths

- A millimetre is a tenth of a centimetre (10 mm = 1 cm)
- A centimetre is a tenth of a decimetre (10 cm = 1 dm)
- A decimetre is a tenth of a metre (10 dm = 1 m)
- A centimetre is a hundredth of a metre (100 cm = 1 m)

Decimals are short forms for fractions. The chart shows the value of the decimal digits.

1. Write the place value of the underlined digit.

a) 2.6<u>3</u>   hundredths

b) 3.<u>2</u>1

c) <u>7</u>.52

d) 5.<u>2</u>9

e) 9.9<u>8</u>

f) <u>1</u>.05

g) <u>0</u>.32

h) 5.5<u>5</u>

i) 6.<u>4</u>2

2. Give the place value of the number 7 in each of the numbers below.

a) 2.73

b) 9.73

c) 0.47

d) 2.07

e) 0.07

f) 7.83

g) 9.75

h) 2.37

i) 6.67

3. Write the following numbers into the place value chart.

	Ones	Tenths	Hundredths
a) 6.02	6	0	2
b) 8.36			
c) 0.25			
d) 1.20			
e) 0.07			

1. Count the number of shaded squares. Write a fraction for the shaded part of the hundreds square.
   Then write the fraction as a decimal.

   HINT: Count by 10s for each column or row that is shaded.

a)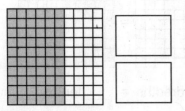

b)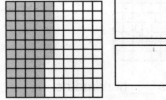

c)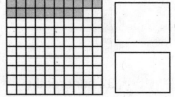

d)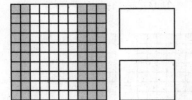

e)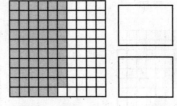

f)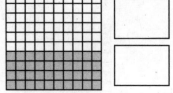

g)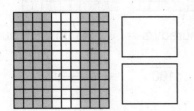

h)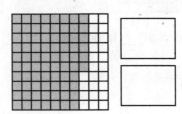

i)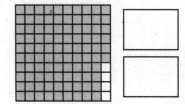

2. Convert the fraction to a decimal. Then shade.

a) $\dfrac{38}{100}$ =

b) $\dfrac{45}{100}$ =

c) $\dfrac{5}{100}$ =

3. Write a fraction and a decimal for
   each shaded part.

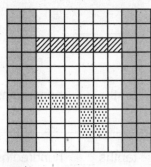

4. Choose 3 designs of your own. Write a fraction
   and a decimal for each shaded part.

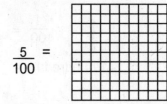

jump math
MULTIPLYING POTENTIAL

Number Sense 2

NS4-102: Tenths and Hundredths

1. Write a fraction and a decimal to represent the number of shaded squares.

a)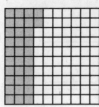

32 hundredths = 3 tenths ___ hundredths

$$\frac{32}{100} = .\underline{\ 3\ }\ \underline{\ 2\ }$$

b)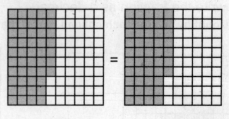

___ hundredths = ___ tenths ___ hundredths

$$\frac{}{100} = .\underline{\ \ }\ \underline{\ \ }$$

c)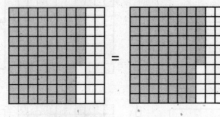

___ hundredths = ___ tenths ___ hundredths

$$\frac{}{100} = .\underline{\ \ }\ \underline{\ \ }$$

d)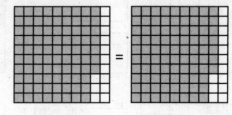

___ hundredths = ___ tenths ___ hundredths

$$\frac{}{100} = .\underline{\ \ }\ \underline{\ \ }$$

2. Fill in the blanks.

a) 71 hundredths = ___ tenths ___ hundredth

$$\frac{71}{100} = .\underline{\ 7\ }\ \underline{\ 1\ }$$

b) 28 hundredths = ___ tenths ___ hundredths

$$\frac{}{100} = .\underline{\ \ }\ \underline{\ \ }$$

c) 41 hundredths = ___ tenths ___ hundredth

$$\frac{}{100} = .\underline{\ \ }\ \underline{\ \ }$$

d) 60 hundredths = ___ tenths ___ hundredths

$$\frac{}{100} = .\underline{\ \ }\ \underline{\ \ }$$

e) 8 hundredths = ___ tenths ___ hundredths

$$\frac{}{100} = .\underline{\ \ }\ \underline{\ \ }$$

f) 2 hundredths = ___ tenths ___ hundredths

$$\frac{}{100} = .\underline{\ \ }\ \underline{\ \ }$$

3. Describe each decimal in two ways.

a) .52 = _5_ tenths _2_ hundredths

  = ___52 hundredths___

b) .83 = ___ tenths ___ hundredths

  = _____

c) .24 = ___ tenths ___ hundredths

  = _____

d) .70 = ___ tenths ___ hundredths

  = _____

e) .07 = ___ tenths ___ hundredths

  = _____

f) .02 = ___ tenths ___ hundredths

  = _____

1. Fill in the chart below. The first one has been done for you.

Drawing	Fraction	Decimal	Equivalent Decimal	Equivalent Fraction	Drawing
	$\frac{5}{10}$	0.5	0.50	$\frac{50}{100}$	

2. Write a fraction for the number of <u>hundredths</u>. Then count the shaded columns and write a fraction for the number of <u>tenths</u>.

a)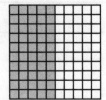

$\overline{100} = \overline{10}$

b)

$\overline{100} = \overline{10}$

c)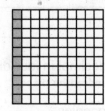

$\overline{100} = \overline{10}$

d)

$\overline{100} = \overline{10}$

3. Fill in the missing numbers.

REMEMBER: $\frac{10}{100} = \frac{1}{10}$

a) $.2 = \frac{2}{10} = \frac{}{100} = .\underline{\ \ }$ b) $.\underline{\ } = \frac{3}{10} = \frac{}{100} = .30$ c) $.\underline{\ } = \frac{7}{10} = \frac{}{100} = .70$

d) $.\underline{\ } = \frac{5}{10} = \frac{}{100} = .\underline{\ \ }$ e) $.\underline{\ } = \frac{}{10} = \frac{60}{100} = .\underline{\ \ }$ f) $.\underline{\ } = \frac{}{10} = \frac{90}{100} = .\underline{\ \ }$

g) $.\underline{\ } = \frac{1}{10} = \frac{}{100} = .\underline{\ \ }$ h) $.\underline{\ } = \frac{8}{10} = \frac{}{100} = .\underline{\ \ }$ i) $.4 = \frac{}{10} = \frac{}{100} = .\underline{\ \ }$

A **dime** is **one tenth** of a dollar. A **penny** is one **hundredth** of a dollar.

1. Express the value of each decimal in four different ways.

   a) .73

   _____ 7 dimes 3 pennies _____

   _____ 7 tenths 3 hundredths _____

   _____ 73 pennies _____

   _____ 73 hundredths _____

   b) .62

   _____

   _____

   _____

   _____

   c) .48

   _____

   _____

   _____

   _____

   d) .03

   _____

   _____

   _____

   _____

   e) .09

   _____

   _____

   _____

   f) .19

   _____

   _____

   _____

2. Express the value of each decimal in four different ways.
   HINT: First add a zero in the hundredths place.

   a) .6   _____ dimes _____ pennies

   _____ tenths _____ hundredths

   _____ pennies

   _____ hundredths

   b) .8   _____ dimes _____ pennies

   _____ tenths _____ hundredths

   _____ pennies

   _____ hundredths

3. Express the value of each decimal in four different ways. Then circle the greater number.

   a) .3   _____ dimes _____ pennies

   _____ tenths _____ hundredths

   _____ pennies

   _____ hundredths

   b) .18   _____ dimes _____ pennies

   _____ tenths _____ hundredths

   _____ pennies

   _____ hundredths

4. Fred says .32 is greater than .5 because 32 is greater than 5. Can you explain his mistake?

![jump math] MULTIPLYING POTENTIAL.

Number Sense 2

1. Fill in the missing numbers.

   a) 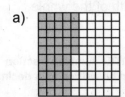   b) 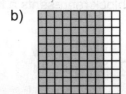   c) 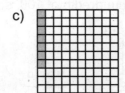   d)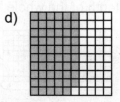

tenths	hundredths

tenths	hundredths

tenths	hundredths

tenths	hundredths

$\overline{100}$ = . $\underset{\text{tenths}}{\_\_\_}$ $\underset{\text{hundredths}}{\_\_\_}$ $\overline{100}$ = . $\_\_\_$ $\_\_\_$ $\overline{100}$ = . $\_\_\_$ $\_\_\_$ $\overline{100}$ = . $\_\_\_$ $\_\_\_$

2. Write the following decimals as fractions.

   a) $.7 = \overline{10}$ b) $.3 = \overline{10}$ c) $.5 = \overline{10}$ d) $.1 = \overline{10}$ e) $.9 = \overline{10}$

   f) $.23 = \overline{100}$ g) $.48 = \overline{100}$ h) $.66 = \overline{100}$ i) $.73 = \overline{100}$ j) $.29 = \overline{100}$

   k) $.07 = \overline{100}$ l) $.02 = \overline{100}$ m) $.09 = \overline{100}$ n) $.01 = \overline{100}$ o) $.04 = \overline{100}$

   p) $.7 =$ q) $.8 =$ r) $.05 =$ s) $.7 =$ t) $.07 =$

   u) $.2 =$ v) $.35 =$ w) $.04 =$ x) $.8 =$ y) $.6 =$

   z) $.02 =$ aa) $.72 =$ bb) $.4 =$ cc) $.23 =$ dd) $.25 =$

3. Change the following fractions to decimals.

   a) $\frac{6}{10} = .\_\_$ b) $\frac{3}{10} = .\_\_$ c) $\frac{4}{10} = .\_\_$ d) $\frac{8}{10} = .\_\_$

   e) $\frac{82}{100} = .\_\_\_$ f) $\frac{7}{100} = .\_\_\_$ g) $\frac{77}{100} = .\_\_\_$ h) $\frac{9}{100} = .\_\_\_$

4. Circle the equalities that are incorrect.

   $.52 = \frac{52}{100}$ $.8 = \frac{8}{10}$ $.5 = \frac{5}{100}$ $\frac{17}{100} = .17$ $\frac{3}{100} = .03$

   $.7 = \frac{7}{100}$ $.53 = \frac{53}{10}$ $.64 = \frac{64}{100}$ $.05 = \frac{5}{100}$ $.02 = \frac{2}{10}$

A hundreds block may be used to represent a whole. 10 is a tenth of 100, so a tens block represents a tenth of the whole. 1 is a hundredth of 100, so a ones block represents a hundredth of the whole.

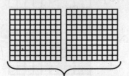   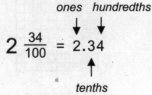

2 wholes   3 tenths   4 hundredths

ones   hundredths

$$2 \frac{34}{100} = 2.34$$

tenths

NOTE: A mixed fraction can be written as a decimal.

----

1. Write a mixed fraction and a decimal for the base ten models below.

a)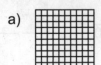

b)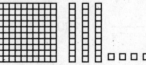

c)

d)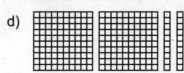

e)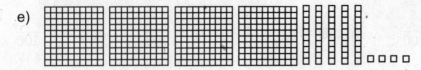

2. Draw a base ten model for the following decimals.

   a) 3.21   b) 1.62

3. Write a decimal and a mixed fraction for each of the pictures below.

a)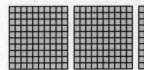

b)

4. Write a decimal for each of the mixed fractions below.

   a) $1 \frac{32}{100} =$ b) $2 \frac{71}{100} =$ c) $8 \frac{7}{10} =$ d) $4 \frac{27}{100} =$

   e) $3 \frac{7}{100} =$ f) $17 \frac{8}{10} =$ g) $27 \frac{1}{10} =$ h) $38 \frac{5}{100} =$

5. Which decimal represents a greater number? Explain your answer with a picture.

   a) 6 tenths or 6 hundredths?   b) . 8 or . 08?   c) 1.02 or 1.20?

This number line is divided into tenths.

The number represented by Point A is $2\frac{3}{10}$ or 2.3.

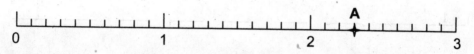

1. Write a decimal and a fraction (or mixed fraction) for each point.

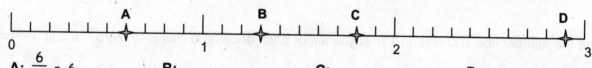

A: $\frac{6}{10}$ = .6   B: _____   C: _____   D: _____

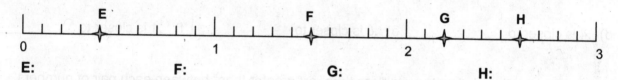

E: _____   F: _____   G: _____   H: _____

2. Mark each point with an 'X' and label the points with the correct letter.

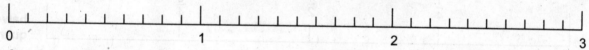

A. 1.1   B. 2.5   C. .60   D. 1.9

E. $1\frac{3}{10}$ F. $2\frac{1}{10}$ G. $1\frac{7}{10}$ H. $\frac{27}{10}$

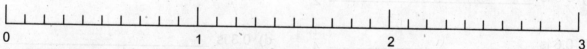

I. five tenths   J. one and six tenths   K. two and four tenths   L. two decimal nine

3. Write the name of each point as a fraction in words (e.g. seven tenths).

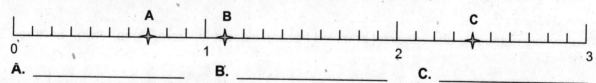

A. _____   B. _____   C. _____

4. Mark the approximate position of each point on the number line.

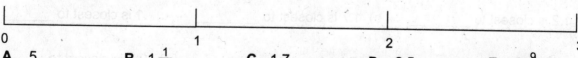

A. .5   B. $1\frac{1}{10}$ C. 1.7   D. 2.5   E. $2\frac{9}{10}$

1.

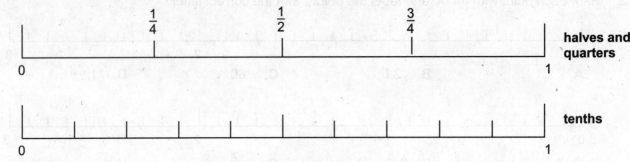

a) Write a decimal for each point marked on the number line. (The first decimal is written for you.)

b) Which decimal is equal to one half? $\frac{1}{2}$ =

2. Use the number line in Question 1 to say whether each decimal is closer to "zero," "a half" or "one."

a) .2 is closer to _____

b) .6 is closer to _____

c) .9 is closer to _____

d) .4 is closer to _____

e) .8 is closer to _____

f) .1 is closer to _____

3. Use the number lines below to write "less than" or "greater than" between each pair of numbers.

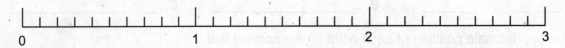

a) 0.3 is _____ $\frac{1}{2}$

b) 0.9 is _____ $\frac{3}{4}$

c) 0.6 is _____ $\frac{1}{4}$

d) 0.3 is _____ $\frac{1}{4}$

e) 0.4 is _____ $\frac{1}{2}$

f) 0.7 is _____ $\frac{3}{4}$

4. Which whole number is each decimal or mixed fraction closest to: "zero," "one," "two," or "three"?

a) 1.2 is closest to _____

b) 1.7 is closest to _____

c) .1 is closest to _____

d) $2\frac{9}{10}$ is closest to _____

e) .7 is closest to _____

f) 2.7 is closest to _____

1. Write the numbers in increasing order. First change each decimal to a fraction with denominator 10.

a) 0.7   0.3   0.5

$\boxed{\dfrac{7}{10}}$ $\boxed{}$ $\boxed{}$

b) $\dfrac{1}{10}$ 0.3   0.9

$\boxed{}$ $\boxed{}$ $\boxed{}$

c) 0.2   0.6 $\dfrac{3}{10}$

$\boxed{}$ $\boxed{}$ $\boxed{}$

_____

d) 1.2   3.5   3.1

$\boxed{1\dfrac{2}{10}}$ $\boxed{}$ $\boxed{}$

e) 1.5   1.2   1.7

$\boxed{}$ $\boxed{}$ $\boxed{}$

f) $1\dfrac{1}{10}$ .7   3.5

$\boxed{}$ $\boxed{}$ $\boxed{}$

_____

g) $1\dfrac{3}{10}$ 1.2   1.1

$\boxed{}$ $\boxed{}$ $\boxed{}$

h) 4.5   3.2 $1\dfrac{7}{10}$

$\boxed{}$ $\boxed{}$ $\boxed{}$

i) 2.3   2.9 $2\dfrac{1}{2}$

$\boxed{}$ $\boxed{}$ $\boxed{}$

_____

2. Karen says: "To compare .6 and .42, I add a zero to .6.

.6 = 6 tenths = 60 hundredths = .60

60 (hundredths) is greater than 42 (hundredths).

So .6 is greater than .42."

Add a zero to the decimal expressed in tenths. Then circle the greater number in each pair.

a) .7   .52   b) .34   .6   c) .82   .5

3. Write each decimal as a fraction with denominator 100 by first adding a zero to the decimal.

a) .7 = $\boxed{.70}$ = $\boxed{\dfrac{70}{100}}$ b) .6 = $\boxed{}$ = $\boxed{}$ c) .5 = $\boxed{}$ = $\boxed{}$

4. Write the numbers in order from least to greatest by first changing all of the decimals to fractions with denominator 100.

a) .2   .8   .35

$\boxed{\dfrac{20}{100}}$ $\boxed{}$ $\boxed{}$

b) $\dfrac{27}{100}$ .9   .25

$\boxed{}$ $\boxed{}$ $\boxed{}$

c) 1.3 $1\dfrac{22}{100}$ $1\dfrac{39}{100}$

$\boxed{}$ $\boxed{}$ $\boxed{}$

_____

5. 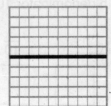 Shade $\frac{1}{2}$ of the squares. Write 2 fractions and 2 decimals for $\frac{1}{2}$.

Fractions: $\frac{1}{2}$ = $\frac{}{10}$ = $\frac{}{100}$

Decimals: $\frac{1}{2}$ = .____ = .____

6.  Shade $\frac{1}{5}$ of the boxes. Write 2 fractions and 2 decimals for $\frac{1}{5}$.

Fractions: $\frac{1}{5}$ = $\frac{}{10}$ = $\frac{}{100}$

Decimals: $\frac{1}{5}$ = .____ = .____

7. Write equivalent fractions.

a) $\frac{2}{5}$ = $\frac{}{10}$ = $\frac{}{100}$ b) $\frac{3}{5}$ = $\frac{}{10}$ = $\frac{}{100}$ c) $\frac{4}{5}$ = $\frac{}{10}$ = $\frac{}{100}$

8. 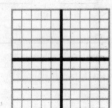 Shade $\frac{1}{4}$ of the squares. Write a fraction and a decimal for $\frac{1}{4}$.

Fraction: $\frac{1}{4}$ = $\frac{}{100}$ *Decimal:* $\frac{1}{4}$ = .____

9. Circle the greater number.

HINT: First change all fractions and decimals to fractions with denominator 100.

a) $\frac{1}{2}$ .37   b) $\frac{1}{4}$ .52   c) $\frac{2}{5}$ .42

d) .7 $\frac{3}{5}$ e) .23 $\frac{1}{5}$ f) .52 $\frac{1}{2}$

 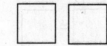

10. Write the numbers in order from least to greatest by first changing all fractions and decimals to fractions with denominator 100.

a) .7   .32 $\frac{1}{2}$ b) $\frac{1}{4}$ $\frac{3}{5}$ .63   c) $\frac{2}{5}$ .35 $\frac{1}{2}$

_____   _____   _____

NS4-110: Adding and Subtracting Tenths

1. 1.3 is one whole and 3 tenths. How many tenths is that altogether? _____

2 a) 4.7 = _____ tenths   b) 7. 1 = _____ tenths   c) 3. 0 = _____ tenths

   d) _____ = 38 tenths   e) _____ = 42 tenths   f) _____ = 7 tenths

3. Add or subtract the decimals by first writing them as whole numbers of tenths.

a)	2.1	_21_ tenths	b)	1.3	___ tenths	c)	1.4	___ tenths
+	1.0	_10_ tenths	+	1.1	___ tenths	+	7.3	___ tenths
	3.1	← _31_ tenths			← ___ tenths			← ___ tenths

d)	2.5	___ tenths	e)	7.6	___ tenths	f)	8.9	___ tenths
−	1.0	___ tenths	−	4.2	___ tenths	−	1.4	___ tenths
		← ___ tenths			← ___ tenths			← ___ tenths

4. Find the sum or difference.

a)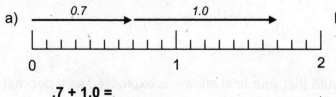

.7 + 1.0 = _____

b)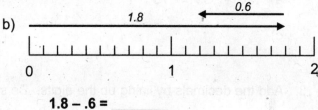

1.8 − .6 = _____

Now draw your own arrows.

c)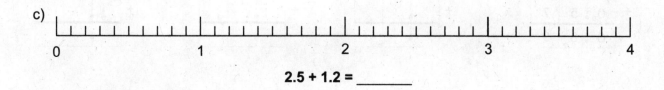

2.5 + 1.2 = _____

d)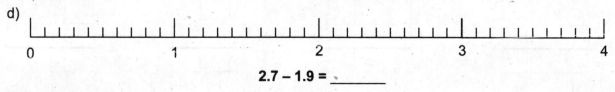

2.7 − 1.9 = _____

5. Add or subtract.

a)	3.5	b)	4.6	c)	5.4	d)	9.2	e)	3.7	f)	2.8
−	1.2	+	3.2	+	1.7	−	4.9	+	4.9	−	1.9

jump math
MULTIPLYING POTENTIAL

Number Sense 2

1. Write a fraction for each shaded part. Then add the fractions together and shade your answer. The first one has been done for you.

a) + = 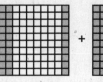   b) + =

$$\frac{20}{100} + \frac{55}{100} = \frac{75}{100}$$ + =

c) + 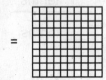 = 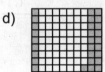   d) + =

2. Write the decimals that correspond to the fractions in Question 1.

a) .20 + .55 = .75   b)

c)   d)

3. Add the decimals by lining up the digits. Be sure that your final answer is expressed as a decimal.

a) 0.32 + 0.57   b) 0.92 + 0.05   c) 0.54 + 0.27   d) 0.22 + 0.75

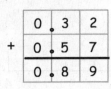   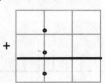   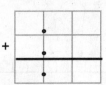   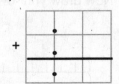

e) 0.7 + 0.25   f) 0.3 + 0.87   g) 0.72 + 0.31   h) 0.38 + 0.52

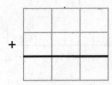   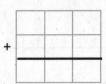   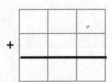   

4. Add the following decimals.

a) 0.32 + 0.17 =   b) 0.64 + 0.23 =   c) 0.46 + 0.12=   d) 0.87 + 0.02 =

e) 0.94 + 0.03 =   f) 0.19 + 0.61=   g) 0.67 + 0.2 =   h) 0.48 + 0.31 =

NS4-112: Subtracting Hundredths

1. Subtract by crossing out the correct number of boxes.

a)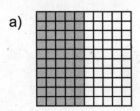

$\dfrac{50}{100} - \dfrac{20}{100} =$ _____

b)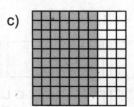

$\dfrac{38}{100} - \dfrac{25}{100} =$ _____

c)

$\dfrac{69}{100} - \dfrac{42}{100} =$ _____

2. Write the decimals that correspond to the fractions in Question 1 above.

a) .50 - .20 = .30   b)   c)

3. Subtract the decimals by lining up the digits. Regroup where necessary.

a) 0.53 − 0.21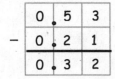

b) 0.93 − 0.31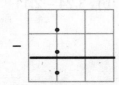

c) 0.87 − 0.26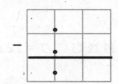

d) 0.39 − 0.11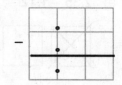

e) 0.67 − 0.59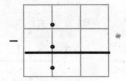

f) 0.23 − 0.19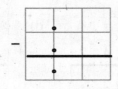

g) 0.74 − 0.59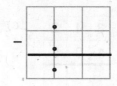

h) 0.93 − 0.18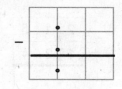

i) 1.00 − 0.46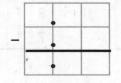

j) 1.00 − 0.26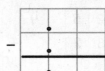

k) 1.00 − 0.57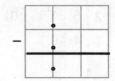

l) 1.00 − 0.89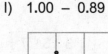

4. Subtract the following decimals.

a) .52 − .43   b) .98 − .36   c) .75 − .47   d) .32 − .29

e) .58 − .5   f) .63 − .3   g) .89 − .07   h) .41 − .08

5. Find the missing decimal in each of the following.

a) 1 = .45 + ☐   b) 1 = .63 + ☐   c) 1 = .39 + ☐

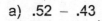

jump math
MULTIPLYING POTENTIAL.

Number Sense 2

1. Add by drawing a base ten model. (Use a hundred block for a whole) Then, line up the numbers and add

   a) 1.23 + 1.12

   b) 1.14 + 1.21

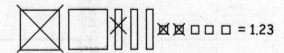

ones	tenths	hundredths
+		

ones	tenths	hundredths
+		

2. Subtract by drawing a base ten model of the greater number as shown in part a).

   a) 2.35 – 1.12

   b) 3.24 – 2.11

⊠ ☐ |╳|| ⊠⊠ ☐ ☐ ☐ = 1.23

3. Add or subtract. In some questions, you will need to regroup.

   a)
   ```
     2 . 1 5
   + 1 . 2 4
   ---------
   ```

   b)
   ```
     3 . 4 2
   + 1 . 0 5
   ---------
   ```

   c)
   ```
     2 . 7 1
   + 1 . 4 2
   ---------
   ```

   d)
   ```
     3 . 8 7
   + 2 . 9 3
   ---------
   ```

   e)
   ```
     5 . 3 2
   + 3 . 1 9
   ---------
   ```

   f)
   ```
     3 . 3 7
   - 1 . 2 4
   ---------
   ```

   g)
   ```
     2 . 5 1
   - 1 . 4 0
   ---------
   ```

   h)
   ```
     4 . 2 5
   - 1 . 8 2
   ---------
   ```

   i)
   ```
     8 . 3 2
   - 1 . 5 3
   ---------
   ```

   j)
   ```
     9 . 7 5
   - 7 . 1 6
   ---------
   ```

4. The largest animal heart measured belonged to a blue whale.
   It weighed 698.5 kg.
   How much would two hearts of that size weigh?

5. The world record for longest hair is 7.5 m.
   Julia's hair is .37 m long.
   How much longer than Julia's hair is the longest hair?

1. Fill in the blanks.

a) .53 + .1 = _____   b) .23 + .1 = _____   c) .07 + .1 = _____

d) .59 + .1 = _____   e) .84 + .01 = _____   f) .30 + .01 = _____

g) 3.75 + .01 = _____   h) 4.63 + .1 = _____   i) 5.98 + .01 = _____

2. Fill in the blanks.

a) _____ is .1 more than .8   b) _____ is .1 more than 3.7

c) _____ is .1 more than .3   d) _____ is .1 more than .52

e) _____ is .1 more than .7   f) _____ is .1 more than .29

3. Fill in the blanks.

a) 1.35 + _____ = 1.36   b) 2.3 + _____ = 2.4   c) 3.06 − _____ = 3.05

d) 4.95 − _____ = 4.94   e) 3.7 + _____ = 4.7   f) 7.85 + _____ = 7.95

g) 9.08 + _____ = 9.18   h) 2.31 − _____ = 2.21   i) 5.01 − _____ = 5.00

4. Fill in the missing numbers on the number lines.

a)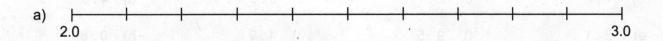
2.0   3.0

b)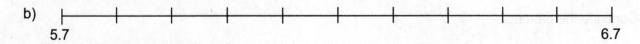
5.7   6.7

5. Continue the patterns.

a) .3, .4, .5, _____, _____, _____   b) 1.4, 1.5, 1.6, _____, _____, _____

c) 2.6, 2.7, 2.8, _____, _____, _____   d) 5.5, 5.6, 5.7, _____, _____, _____

6. Fill in the blanks.

a) 2.9 + .1 = _____   b) 7.9 + .1 = _____   c) 6.95 + .1 = _____

1. Read the numbers from left to right and circle the first place value where they differ. Then write the greater number in the box.

a)   3 . 2 5
    3 . 3 8

   | 3 . 3 8 |

b)   7 . 0 4
    7 . 0 6

c)   8 . 5 3
    8 . 4 2

d)   9 . 2
    9 . 1 5

e)   6 . 3 5
    6 . 4

2. Write < or > to show the greater number.

a) 5 . 2 5 | > | 5 . 1 3

b) 8 . 3 2 | | 8 . 1 5

c) 7 . 0 5 | | 7 . 0 4

d) 6 . 3 2 | | 5 . 7 0

e) 4 . 3 | | 4 . 1 2

f) 6 . 2 1 | | 6.4

3. Using the numbers 1, 2, 3, 4 create …

a) the greatest number.

   ☐ ☐ . ☐ ☐

b) the least number.

   ☐ ☐ . ☐ ☐

4. Write three decimals greater than .4 and less than .5: _____ _____ _____

5. Round the numbers to the nearest whole number.

a) 1 . 7

b) 2 . 1

c) 3 . 9

d) 4 . 3

e) 8 . 1

f) 9 . 5

g) 4 . 9

h) 0 . 8

6. Continue the patterns.

a) .2 , .4 , .6 , _____ , _____

b) .3 , .6 , .9 , _____ , _____

7. Explain the error:

      5.2
  + 3 . 4 2
    3 . 9 4

8. Explain why 1.02 is less than 1.20.

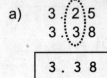

jump math
MULTIPLYING POTENTIAL

Number Sense 2

1. Draw a picture in the space provided to show 1 tenth of each whole.

a)

    1 whole   1 tenth

b)

    1 whole   1 tenth

c)

    1 whole   1 tenth

The size of a unit of measurement depends on which unit has been selected as the **whole**.

2. Write each measurement as a fraction, then as a decimal.
   REMEMBER: 1 centimetre is 1 hundredth of a metre.

a) 1 cm = $\frac{1}{100}$ m = .01 m

b) 4 cm = _____ m = _____ m

c) 75 cm = _____ m = _____ m

d) 17 cm = _____ m = _____ m

e) 8 mm = $\frac{8}{10}$ cm = _____ cm

f) 7 mm = _____ cm = _____ cm

g) 5 mm = _____ cm = _____ cm

h) 4 mm = _____ cm = _____ cm

3. Add the measurements by first changing the <u>smaller unit</u> into a decimal in the <u>larger unit</u>.

   a) 4 cm + 9.2 m
      = .04 m + 9.2 m
      = 9.24 m

   b) 18 cm + 2.4 m

   c) 6 cm + 8.2 m

   d) 26 cm + 1.52 m

   e) 423 cm + 1.75 m

4.

Plant	Height
Canada Golden Rod	1.5 m
Field Birdwell	1 m
White Sweet Clover	300 cm
Yellow Sorrel	0.5 m

a) How should Rick order the flowers so the shortest are at the front of his garden, and the tallest at the back?

b) How much taller will the clover grow than the sorrei?

5. $0.25 means 2 dimes and 5 pennies.
   Why do we use decimal notation for money?
   What is a dime a tenth of?
   What is a penny a hundredth of?

NS4-117: Dividing by 10 and 100

Example: Divide 40 into 10 sets.
There are 4 in each set.

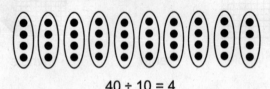

40 ÷ 10 = 4

Divide 40 into steps of size 10.
There are 4 steps.

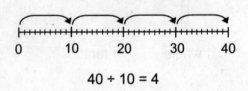

40 ÷ 10 = 4

Similarly, dividing by 100 removes two zeroes. (To see this, divide 200 counters into 100 groups; there will be 2 counters in each group.)

----

1. Group the dots into 10 sets and complete the division statement.

a)

   30 ÷ 10 = _____

b)

   20 ÷ 10 = _____

2. Divide.

   a) 70 ÷ 10 = _____   b) 40 ÷ 10 = _____   c) 60 ÷ 10 = _____   d) 90 ÷ 10 = _____

   e) 280 ÷ 10 = _____   f) 360 ÷ 10 = _____   g) 720 ÷ 10 = _____   h) 1250 ÷ 10 = _____

3. Complete each statement.

   a) 300 = 100 × 3   b) 400 = 100 × 4   c) 900 = 100 × 9

   so ____300 ÷ 100 = 3____   so _____   so _____

4. Divide.

   a) 700 ÷ 100 = _____   b) 800 ÷ 100 = _____   c) 600 ÷ 100 = _____   d) 1800 ÷ 100 = _____

   e) 2000 ÷ 10 = _____   f) 2000 ÷ 100 = _____   g) 9100 ÷ 10 = _____   h) 10000 ÷ 100 = _____

5. Dividing a whole number by 10 shifts the decimal one place.

   Example:

   Divide 2 into 10 parts.

   Each part is .2 units long

   2.0 ÷ 10 = 0.2

   Divide.

   a) 4.0 ÷ 10 = _____   b) 6.0 ÷ 10 = _____   c) 15.0 ÷ 10 = _____

NS4-118: Changing Units

1. Change the amount given from dollars and cents to cents.

   a) 2 dollars 7 cents = _____207 cents_____   b) 5 dollars 21 cents = _____

   c) 6 dollars 4 cents = _____   d) 8 dollars 5 cents = _____

2. Changing the measurement from metres and centimetres to centimetres.

   a) 3 m 2 cm = _____302 cm_____   b) 4 m 9 cm = _____   c) 2 m 19 cm = _____

   d) 8 m 10 cm = _____   e) 17 m 30 cm = _____   f) 1 m 1 cm = _____

BONUS
3. Change the measurement from kilometres and metres to metres.

   a) 7 km 2 m = _____7002 m_____   b) 2 km 36 m = _____   c) 8 km 7 m = _____

   d) 6 km 3 m = _____   e) 4 km 125 m = _____   f) 13 km 1 m = _____

4. Change from hours and minutes to minutes. (Remember that there are 60 minutes in an hour.)

   a) 3 h 7 min = _____187 min_____   b) 1 h 8 min = _____   c) 2 h 5 min = _____

   d) 2 h 17 min = _____   e) 2 h 45 min = _____   f) 3 h 20 min = _____

5. Change each amount to a decimal form (in the larger unit).

   a) $3 and 5¢ = _____$3.05_____   b) $7 and 8¢ = _____   c) $12 and 17¢ = _____

   d) 4 m 7 cm = _____   e) 5 m 9 cm = _____   f) 10 m 27 cm = _____

Answer the following questions in your notebook.

1. From the diagram, you can see that 2 × 4 = 4 × 2.

   a) Show with a diagram that 3 × 5 = 5 × 3.

   b) If A and B are whole numbers,
      is it always true that A × B = B × A?
      Explain.

   2 rows of 4:

   4 rows of 2:

   2 × 4

   4 × 2

2.   4 × 25 = 100 ,   2 × 50 = 100 ,   4 × 250 = 1000 ,   and   2 × 500 = 1000.

   Knowing the facts above, find the products below by grouping the numbers in a clever way.

   Example: 4 × 18 × 25
                = 4 × 25 × 18
                = 100 × 18
                = 1 800

   a) 2 × 27 × 50   b) 4 × 75 × 250   c) 2 × 97 × 500
   d) 372 × 4 × 25   e) 2 × 2 × 17 × 250   f) 25 × 2 × 50 × 4

3. 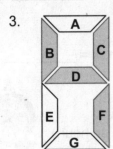 On a digital watch, numbers are made from bars in the shape of trapezoids.
   The number 4 (see picture) is made from the trapezoids B, D, C and F.

   a) List the trapezoids that are needed to make each number from 0 to 9.

   b) Which trapezoid is used most often?

4. a) You can count the dots in an array by grouping them in Ls as shown below.
      Write an addition statement and a multiplication statement for the third array below.

   Addition statement: 1 + 3 = 4   1 + 3 + 5 = 9   _____

   Multiplication statement: 2 × 2 = 4   3 × 3 = 9   _____

   b) Draw a 5-by-5 array and then draw Ls to group the dots.
       Write an addition statement and a multiplication statement for the array.
       Are the numbers in your statement all odd or all even?

   c) How can you find 1 + 3 + 5 + 7 + 9 + 11 without adding?
       HINT: Can you write an equivalent multiplication statement?

Answer the following questions in your notebook.

1. A box of 2 crayons costs 10¢.
   A box of 3 costs 12¢.
   What is the cheapest way
   to buy 6 crayons?

2. Carol had $10.00.
   She spent half her money on a diary.
   Then she spent $1.25 for a pen.
   How much money does she have left?

3. A tray of 4 plants costs 60¢.
   A tray of 6 plants costs 80¢.
   What is the cheapest way to buy 24 plants?
   What strategy did you use to solve the puzzle?

4. Henry is 4 years older than Jane.
   The sum of their ages is 12.
   How old is Henry?

5. A school has 150 students.

   a) 80 of the students are boys. How many are girls?

   b) Each class has 25 students. How many classes are there?

   c) Each class has one teacher.
      The school also has a principal, a vice-principal and a secretary.
      In total, how many adults work at the school? **HINT: Use your answer from b).**

   d) One day, 2 students from each class were sick and didn't come to school.
      How many students were missing that day?

   e) On that same day, how many students were at school?

6. A clothing store has a total of 500 shirts.
   In one week, they sold:
   20 red shirts, 50 blue shirts, and 100 green shirts.
   How many shirts were <u>left</u>
   at the end of the week?

7. In 2004, the winner of the Olympic medal
   in shot put had a throw of 21.16 m.
   The bronze medal throw was 21.07 m.
   How much longer was the gold medal
   throw?

8. Emma ran .55 km along one road
   and .47 km along another road.
   How far did she run?

9. A 2 m long snake was only .2 m at birth.
   How many centimetres
   did the snake grow?

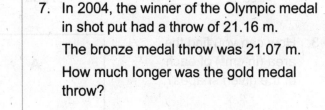

ME4-30: Area in Square Centimetres

Shapes that are flat are called **two-dimensional** (2-D) shapes.

The **area** of a 2-dimensional shape is the amount of space it takes up.

A **square centimetre** is a unit for measuring area.
A square with sides 1 cm has an area of one square centimetre.
The short form for square centimetre is cm².

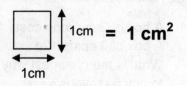

1cm = **1 cm²**

---

1. Find the area of these figures in square centimetres.

   a)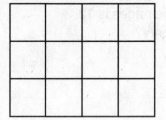

   Area = _____ cm²

   b)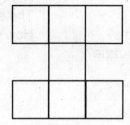

   Area = _____ cm²

   c)

   Area = _____ cm²

2. Using a ruler, join the marks lines to divide each rectangle into square centimetres.

   a)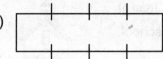

   Area = _____ cm²

   b)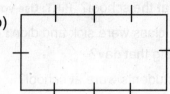

   Area = _____ cm²

   c)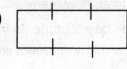

   Area = _____ cm²

3. How can you find the area (in cm²) of each of the given shapes?

   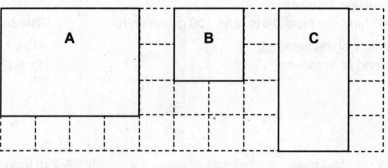

   Area of A = _____   Area of B = _____   Area of C = _____

 4. Draw three different shapes that have an area of 8 cm² (the shapes don't have to be rectangles).

5. Draw several shapes and find their area and perimeter.

6. Draw a rectangle with an area of 8 cm² and perimeter of 12 cm.

 jump math
MULTIPLYING POTENTIAL.

Measurement 2

ME4-31: Area of Rectangles

1. Write a multiplication statement for each array.

   a) 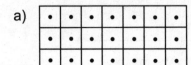   b) 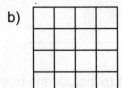   c)   d)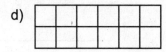

   _____   _____   _____   _____

2. Draw a dot in each box.
   Then write a multiplication statement that tells you the number of boxes in the rectangle.

   a) 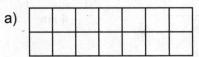   b)   c)   d)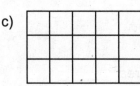

   ___3 × 7 = 21___   _____   _____   _____

3. Write the number of boxes along the width and length of each rectangle.
   Then write a multiplication statement for the area of the rectangle (in square units).

   a) 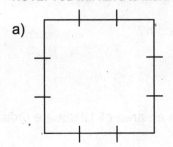   Width
   = ____

   Length = ____

   b) 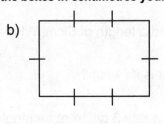   Width
   = ____

   Length = ____

   c)    Width
   = ____

   Length = ____

   _____   _____   _____

4. Using a ruler, join the marks to divide each rectangle into squares.
   Write a multiplication statement for the area of the boxes in cm².
   NOTE: You will have to mark two of the boxes in centimetres yourself, using a ruler.

   a) 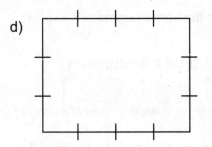   b)   c)

   d)   e)

5. If you know the length and width of a rectangle, how can you find its area? _____

   _____

ME4-32: Exploring Area

1. Measure the length and width of the figures then find the area. Do not forget the units!

   a)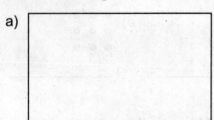

   b)

   c)

   _____   _____   _____

2. a) Calculate the area of each rectangle (be sure to include the units).

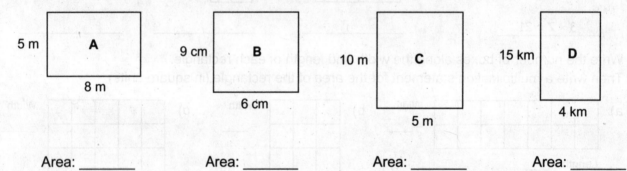

   5 m [A] 8 m

   9 cm [B] 6 cm

   10 m [C] 5 m

   15 km [D] 4 km

   Area: _____   Area: _____   Area: _____   Area: _____

   b) List the rectangles from greatest to least area: _____ , _____ , _____ , _____

3. Find the area of the rectangle with the following dimensions.

   a) width: 5 m   length: 7 m   b) width: 2 m   length: 9 m   c) width: 6 cm   length: 8 cm

4. A rectangle has an area of 10 cm^2 and a length of 5 cm. What is its width?

5. A square has an area of 9 cm^2. What is its width?

6. a) Using grid paper or a geoboard, create 3 different rectangles with an area of 12 square units.

   b) Do all the rectangles have the same perimeter? Explain.

7.
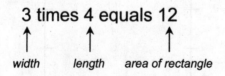

   3 times 4 equals 12

   width   length   area of rectangle

   a) Find a different pair of numbers that multiply to equal 12.

   b) Draw a rectangle with width and length equal to your numbers.

1. Two half squares cover the same area as a whole square .

Count each <u>pair</u> of half squares as a whole square to find the area shaded.

a)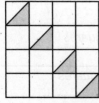

= __3__ whole squares

b)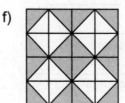

= _____ whole squares

c)

= _____ whole squares

d)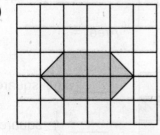

= _____ whole squares

e)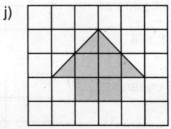

= _____ whole squares

f)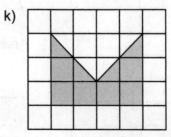

= _____ whole squares

g)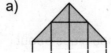

= _____ whole squares

h)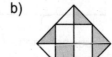

= _____ whole squares

i)

= _____ whole squares

j)

= _____ whole squares

k)

= _____ whole squares

2. Find the answer by dividing the number of half squares by two.

a) 6 half squares = _____ whole squares

b) 8 half squares = _____ whole squares

c) 4 whole squares and 4 half squares = _____ whole squares

3. Is the shaded area more than, less than or equal to the unshaded area? Explain.

a)

b)

4. It took George one hour to paint the part of the house that is shaded. How long will it take him to paint the rest? How do you know? Explain.

a)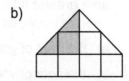

b)

Measurement 2

ME4-34: Finding and Estimating Area

1. The shaded shapes below all represent $\frac{1}{2}$ a square. How many squares do they add up to in total?

a)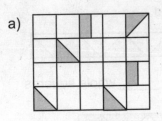

_____
half squares

_____
total squares

b)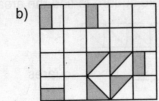

_____
half squares

_____
total squares

c)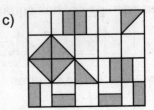

_____
half squares

_____
total squares

2. Fill in the blanks to find the total area.

a)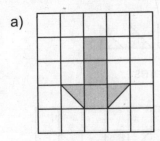

_____3_____ full squares

+ ___2___ $\frac{1}{2}$ squares

= ___4___ full squares

Area = 3 + 1 = 4

b)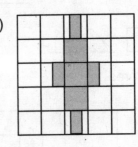

_____ full squares

+ _____ $\frac{1}{2}$ squares

= _____ full squares

Area =

c)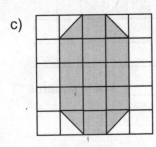

_____ full squares

+ _____ $\frac{1}{2}$ squares

= _____ full squares

Area =

d)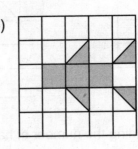

_____ full squares

+ _____ $\frac{1}{2}$ squares

= _____ full squares

Area =

3.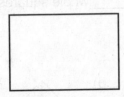

The area of your thumbnail is about 1 square centimetre (1 cm^2).
Estimate the area of this rectangle using your thumbnail.
Then measure the sides of the rectangle and find its actual area.

4. A square metre (1 m^2) has sides about as long as your arm span.
Say whether each object below has surface area greater than or less than 1 m^2.
Then estimate its area.

a) the seat of your chair

b) the floor of your class

c) the surface of the blackboard

5. Estimate the area of the lake by counting whole and half squares.
NOTE: Each square represents 1 km^2.

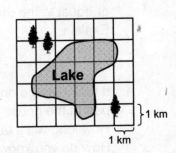

Lake

1 km
1 km

ME4-35: Comparing Area and Perimeter

1. Record the perimeter and area of each shape in the chart below.
   NOTE: Each square represents a square centimetre.

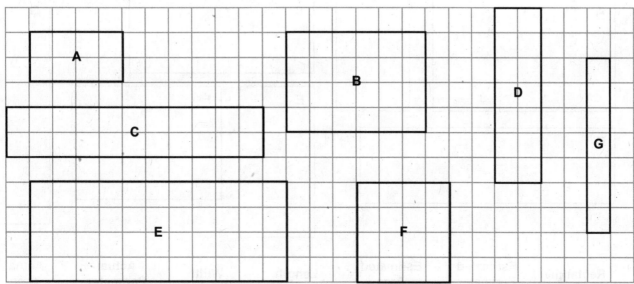

Shape	Perimeter	Area
A	2 + 4 + 2 + 4 = 12 cm	2 x 4 = 8 cm^2
B		
C		
D		
E		
F		
G		

2. Shape C has greater perimeter than shape B. Does it also have a greater area? _____

3. Name two other shapes where one has a greater perimeter and the other has a greater area.

   _____

4. Write the shapes in order from greatest to least perimeter. _____

5. Write the shapes in order from greatest to least area. _____

6. Are the orders in Questions 4 and 5 the same? _____

7. What is the difference between PERIMETER and AREA? _____

   _____

   _____

1. Measure the length and width of each rectangle. Then fill in the chart below.

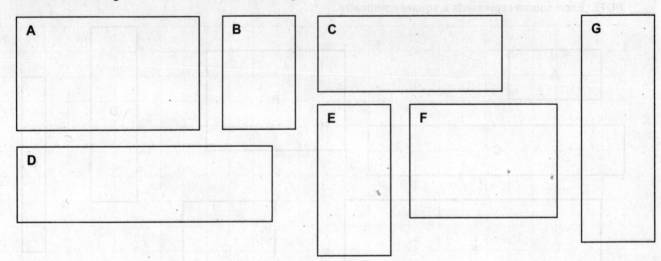

Rectangle	Estimated Perimeter	Estimated Area	Length	Width	Actual Perimeter	Actual Area
A	cm	cm^2	cm	cm	cm	cm^2
B						
C						
D						
E						
F						
G						

2. a) Draw 3 shapes of any kind on grid paper, each with an area of 10 square units.

    b) Do shapes have to be congruent to have the same area?

3. Find the area of the rectangle using the clues. Show your work in your notebook.

    a) Width = 2 cm   Perimeter = 10 cm

        Area = ?

    b) Width = 4 cm   Perimeter = 18 cm

        Area = ?

4. On grid paper, draw a square with the given perimeter. Then find the area of the square.

    a) Perimeter = 12 cm   Area = ?

    b) Perimeter = 20 cm   Area = ?

5. On grid paper draw a figure made of four squares.
    Each square must share at least one edge with
    another square.

    a) How many different figures can you create?

    b) Which figure has the least perimeter?

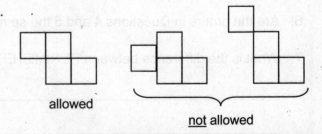

allowed

<u>not</u> allowed

ME4-37: Problems and Puzzles

Answer the questions below in your notebook.

1. On grid paper draw a rectangle with …

   a) an area of 10 square units and a perimeter of 14 units.

   b) an area of 12 square units and a perimeter of 14 units.

2.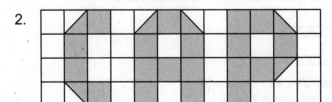

   a) Find the area of the shaded word.

   b) There are 48 squares in the grid.
      How can you use your answer to a) to find the number of <u>unshaded</u> squares?

3. Raj wants to build a rectangular flower bed of width 2 m and perimeter 12 m.

   a) Draw a sketch to show the shape of the flower bed.

   b) What is the length of the bed?

   c) Raj wants to build a fence about the bed.
      If fencing is $7 a metre, how much will this cost?

   d) Raj will plant 4 sunflowers on each square metre of land.
      Each sunflower seed costs 2¢.
      How much will the flowers cost altogether?

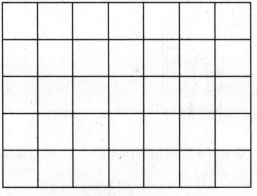

   NOTE: Each edge on the grid
   represents 1 metre.

4. Say whether you would use area or perimeter to measure the following.

   a) The amount of paper needed to cover a bulletin board.

   b) The distance around a field.

   c) The amount of ribbon needed to make a border for a picture.

5. Draw two rectangles to show that figures with the same area can have different perimeters.

Volume is the amount of space taken up by a three dimensional object.

1 cm block

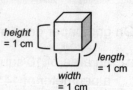

To measure volume, we can use 1 cm blocks. These blocks are uniform squares, with length, width and height all 1 cm long.

The volume of a container is based on how many of these 1 cm blocks will fit inside the container.

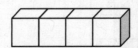

This object, made of centimetre cubes, has a volume of 4 cubes or 4 cubic centimetres (written 4 cm³).

----

1. Using "cubes" as your unit of measurement, write the <u>volume</u> of each object.

a)

Number of cubes _____

b)

Number of cubes _____

c)

Number of cubes _____

d)

Number of cubes _____

e)

Number of cubes _____

f)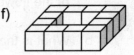

Number of cubes _____

2. Given a structure made of cubes, you can draw a "mat plan" as shown.

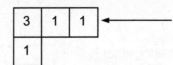

3	1	1
1		

← *The numbers tell you how many cubes are stacked in each position.*

For each figure below, fill in the missing numbers in the mat plan.

a)

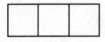

b)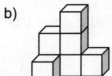

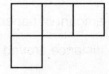

c)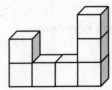

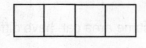

d)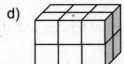

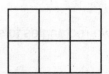

ME4-39: Volume of Rectangular Prisms

1. Use the number of blocks in the shaded column to write an addition statement and a multiplication statement for each area.

a) 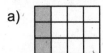 $\underline{3} + \underline{3} + \underline{3} + \underline{3} = \underline{12}$

$\underline{3} \times \underline{4} = \underline{12}$

b) 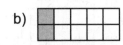 ___ + ___ + ___ + ___ + ___ = ___

___ × ___ = ___

c)  ___ + ___ + ___ + ___ + ___ + ___ + ___ = ___

___ × ___ = ___

2. How many 1 cm³ blocks are in each shaded row? (Blocks are not shown to scale.)

a) 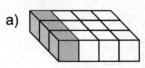   b) 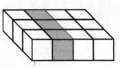   c) 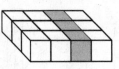   d)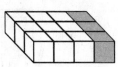

_____ blocks   _____ blocks   _____ blocks   _____ blocks

3. a) Write an addition statement for the volume of the shape.

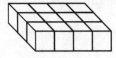   ____ + ____ + ____ + ____ = _____ cm³

b) Write a multiplication statement for the same volume: ____ × ____ = _____ cm³

4. 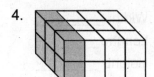 a) How many blocks are shaded? _____

b) Write an addition statement for the volume of the shape.

____ + ____ + ____ + ____ = _____ cm³

c) Write a multiplication statement for the same volume.

____ × 4 = _____ cm³

5. Write an addition and multiplication statement for each volume.

a) 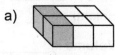   ____ + ____ + ____ = _____ cm³

____ × 3 = _____ cm³

b) 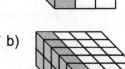   ____ + ____ + ____ + ____ = _____ cm³

____ × ____ = _____ cm³

c) 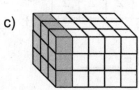   ____ + ____ + ____ + ____ + ____ = _____ cm³

____ × ____ = _____ cm³

jump math
MULTIPLYING POTENTIAL

Measurement 2

6. How many blocks are on the end of each prism?

a)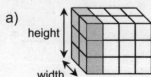

Number of blocks on end

= height × width

= __3__ × __2__ = 6

b)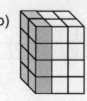

Number of blocks on end

= height × width

= _____ × _____ = 8

c)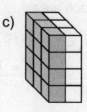

Number of blocks on end

= height × width

= _____ × _____ = 12

7. How many blocks are in each prism?

a)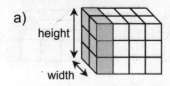

Number of blocks in prism

= height × width × length

= ___ × ___ × ___ = ___

b)

Number of blocks in prism

= height × width × length

= ___ × ___ × ___ = ___

c)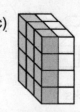

Number of blocks in prism

= height × width × length

= ___ × ___ × ___ = ___

8. Find the volume of each box with the indicated dimensions (assume all units are in metres).

    HINT: V = H × L × W

a)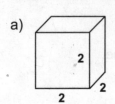

Width: _____
Length: _____
Height: _____

Volume = _____

b)

Width: _____
Length: _____
Height: _____

Volume = _____

c)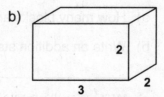

Width: _____
Length: _____
Height: _____

Volume = _____

d)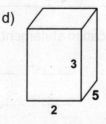

Width: _____
Length: _____
Height: _____

Volume = _____

9. Find the volumes of the rectangular prisms from the mat plans shown below.

a)

5	5	5
5	5	5

W: _____
L: _____
H: _____

Volume = _____

b)

3	3
3	3

W: _____
L: _____
H: _____

Volume = _____

c)

2	2	2	2	2
2	2	2	2	2

W: _____
L: _____
H: _____

Volume = _____

jump math
MULTIPLYING POTENTIAL

ME4-40: Mass

Mass measures the amount of substance in a thing. Grams (g) and kilograms (kg) are units for measuring weight or mass.

One kilogram is equal to 1000 grams.

Things that weigh about one **gram**:
✓ A paper clip
✓ A dime
✓ A chocolate chip

Things that weigh about one **kilogram**:
✓ A one litre bottle of water
✓ A bag of 200 nickels
✓ Two squirrels

---

1. If one paper clip has a weight of approximately one gram, how much would ...

   a) 2 paper clips weigh? _____   b) 8 paper clips weigh? _____

   Now, hold a paper clip in one hand, and your pencil in the other. Think about how many paper clips you would need to balance the weight of the pencil.

   c) About how much does your pencil weigh?   d) About how much does your pen weigh?

2. If a dime has a weight of approximately one gram, how much would ...

   a) 30¢ in dimes weigh? _____   b) 50¢ in dimes weigh? _____   c) 80¢ in dimes weigh? _____

3. Estimate the weight of the following things, in grams.

   a) a chocolate chip cookie _____   b) an apple _____   c) a shoe _____

4. Can you name an object (other than those listed above) that weighs about one gram?

   _____

5. Answer the questions based on the given information on the weight of Canadian coins.
   NOTE: The approximate weights of each coin are given below.

Nickel	4 grams
Dime	2 grams
Quarter	4 grams
Loonie	7 grams

   a) How much would 15¢ in nickels weigh? _____

   b) How much would 9 dimes weigh? _____

   c) How much would $1.00 in quarters weigh? _____

   d) How much would two loonies weigh? _____

   e) How many quarters weigh as much as 6 nickels? _____

   f) Estimate how much a toonie weighs. _____

jump math
MULTIPLYING POTENTIAL

Measurement 2

6. Match the objects on the left with objects on the right that have a similar mass.

7. What unit is more appropriate to measure each item? Circle the appropriate unit.

 grams or kilograms?

 grams or kilograms?

 grams or kilograms?

8. a) Order (by letter) the following from <u>least to greatest</u> mass.

   A. blue whale   **B.** ant   **C.** horse   _____, _____, _____

   b) Order (by letter) the following from <u>greatest to least</u> mass.

   A. 10-year-old human   **B.** house cat   **C.** elephant   _____, _____, _____

9. Check off the appropriate box. Would you use grams or kilograms to weigh ...

   a) a moose? ☐ **g**   ☐ **kg**   b) a desk? ☐ **g**   ☐ **kg**

   c) a piece of cheese? ☐ **g**   ☐ **kg**   d) a tiny bird? ☐ **g**   ☐ **kg**

   e) a pencil? ☐ **g**   ☐ **kg**   f) yourself? ☐ **g**   ☐ **kg**

10. Circle the weight that is more appropriate for the object in the picture.

    a)

    22 kilograms   OR   222 grams

    b)

    130 grams   OR   13 kilograms

11. Write in the missing masses to balance the scales.

    a)

    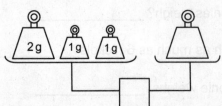

    b)
    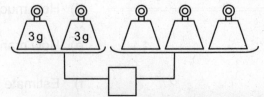

ME4-41: Changing Units of Mass

1. 1 kilogram = 1000 grams   1 kilometre = 1000 metres

    Looking at the equations above, what do you think the Greek word "kilo" means?

2. What do you need to multiply a measurement in kilograms by to change it to grams? _____

3. Change the following measurements to grams.

    a) 3 kg = _____   b) 9 kg = _____   c) 17 kg = _____   d) 25 kg = _____

4. Write an estimate of your weight in kilograms and change your estimate to grams.

5. a) A baby has a mass of 4 000 grams, which is the same as 4 kg.

    Another baby has a mass of 3 000 grams.

    What is its mass in kg? _____

    b) What fact did you use to change grams to kilograms?

6. Circle the greater measure in each pair.
    NOTE: First change both measurements to the same unit.

    a) 25 g   35 g   b) 20 g   17 g   c) 3 kg   5 kg

    d) 50 g   2 kg   e) 400 g   1 kg   f) 2 000 g   1 kg

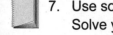

7. Use some of these masses of Antarctic birds to create a problem about mass.
    Solve your problem.

    Emperor Penguin 45 kg; **Adelie Penguin** 6.5 kg; **Giant Antarctic Petrel** 5 kg;
    Cape Petrel 550 g; **Snow Petrel** 300 g.

Answer these problems in your notebook.

1. If a young raccoon weighs two kilograms, how much would …

   a) 3 raccoons weigh?

   b) 7 raccoons weigh?

2. Estimate the weight of the following things in kilograms.

   a) your math book

   b) your desk

   c) a bicycle

3. Jennifer weighed 3 kilograms when she was born.

   She grew at a rate of 200 grams each week.

   How much did Jennifer weigh when she was one month old?

   HINT: First find how many grams she weighed at birth.

4. A male hippo (weighing 1876 kg) and a female hippo (weighing 1347 kg) are walking by a river.

   How much less does the female weigh than the male?

5. Tomato and eggplant seeds weigh 2 grams each.

   Zucchini seeds weigh 3 grams each.

   Daniel bought 12 tomato seeds, 8 eggplant seeds and 5 zucchini seeds.

   How much did his seeds weigh altogether?

6. a) The cost of shipping a package is $2.00 for each kilogram shipped.

      How much does it cost to ship a package that weighs 12 kilograms?

   b) A spoon weighs approximately 60 grams.

      About how much would a set of 6 spoons weigh?

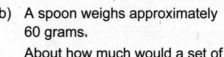

7. A mail carrier is carrying 300 letters in his bag.

   Each letter has a mass of about 20 g.

   Explain how you would find the total mass of the letters.

   c) There are 15 salmon in a pond, and each weighs approximately two kilograms.

      About how much do all the salmon in the pond weigh?

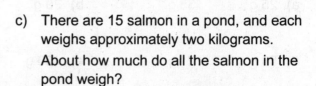

The **capacity** of a container is how much it can hold. The capacity of a regular carton of milk is 1 L.

Litres (L) and millilitres (mL) are the basic units for measuring capacity → 1 litre (L) = 1000 millilitres (mL)

Some sample capacities:

1 teaspoon = 5 mL	1 can of pop = 350 mL	1 regular carton of juice = 1 L
1 tube of toothpaste = 75 mL	1 large bottle of shampoo = 750 mL	1 large can of paint = 3 to 5 L

---

1. Check off the appropriate box. Would you use millilitres (mL) or litres (L) to measure the capacity of ...

   a) a cup of tea? ☐ **mL** ☐ **L**   b) a rain drop? ☐ **mL** ☐ **L**

   c) a bath tub? ☐ **mL** ☐ **L**   d) a bucket of ice cream? ☐ **mL** ☐ **L**

   e) a swimming pool? ☐ **mL** ☐ **L**   f) a medicine bottle? ☐ **mL** ☐ **L**

2. Clare fills a measuring cup with 40 mL of water.
   She pours out some water and notices there
   are 30 mL left.
   How much water did she pour out?

3.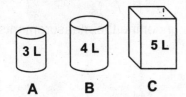

   a) How many containers of size C would hold 20 L?

   b) How many containers of size A would hold as much water as 3 containers of size B?

   c) Which will hold more: 4 containers of size B or 3 containers of size C?

4. How many containers of the given capacity would be needed to make a litre? Explain.

   a) 100 mL   b) 200 mL   c) 500 mL   d) 250 mL

5. Aron filled a large pot with water using a jug with a capacity of 250 mL.
   He filled and emptied the jug 4 times to fill the pot.
   What was the pot's capacity?
   Can you write the capacity in two different ways?

1. Jenna is carrying groceries. In her bag there is ...

- 1 L of milk
- a 500 mL bottle of olive oil
- a 500 mL bottle of vinegar
- a 700 mL jar of tomato sauce

What is the total capacity of the items in mL? _____

2. Circle **true** or **false** for each question below.

a) You would measure the weight of a car in litres.   **True**   **False**

b) A gram is used to measure volume.   **True**   **False**

c) The contents of a can of pop are usually measured in kilograms.   **True**   **False**

d) Grams are used to measure the weight of objects.   **True**   **False**

3. Write a unit of measurement to make each statement reasonable.

a) A tea cup holds about 200 _____ of tea.   b) A chair has a mass of about 4 _____.

c) A house cat weighs over 1000 _____.   d) A bucket holds about 8 _____ of water.

4. For each recipe ...   a) circle the measurements of capacity and underline the measurements
                               of mass.

                           b) total the measurements of mass.

                           c) total the measurements of capacity.

Ice Cream	**Tomato Sauce**	**Birthday Cake**
1 L fresh fruit	30 mL olive oil	115 g butter
50 mL lemon juice	800 mL can of tomatoes	300 g sugar
250 mL heavy cream	30 mL tomato paste	2 eggs
250 mL light cream	5 g fresh oregano	280 g flour
150 g sugar	2 g fresh basil	150 mL milk

Mass: _____   Mass: _____   Mass: _____

Capacity: _____   Capacity: _____   Capacity: _____

ME4-45: Temperature

Degree Celsius is a unit of measurement for temperature. It is written: °C.

Water freezes at 0°C. Water boils at 100°C. The temperature of the human body is 37°C.

----

1. Read the thermometers and record the temperature:

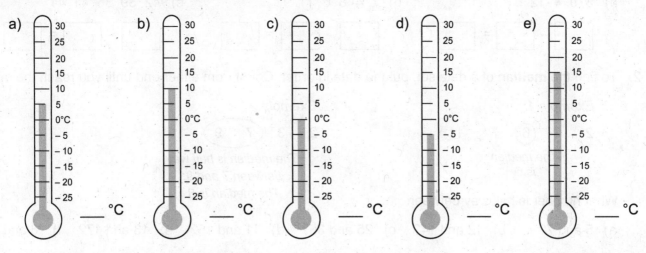

a) ___ °C   b) ___ °C   c) ___ °C   d) ___ °C   e) ___ °C

2. What is the normal temperature range of each season where you live?
    HINT: Ask your teacher for help with this.

    a) Winter –
        between _____ °C and _____ °C

    b) Spring –
        between _____ °C and _____ °C

    c) Summer –
        between _____ °C and _____ °C

    d) Fall –
        between _____ °C and _____ °C

3. Kyle's temperature is 38°C. How much higher is his temperature than normal?

4. Philip is heating water for soup. The temperature of the water is 75°C. How many more degrees must the temperature rise before the water boils?

BONUS
5. Chloe measured the temperature one day and found it was –5°C. The next day, the temperature was 10°C. How many degrees did the temperature rise?

PDM4-13: Range and Median

The **range** of a data set is the difference
between the largest and the smallest data.   *Example:*   The range of 3 7 9 4 is 9 – 3 = 6.

- -

1. Find the range of each data set.

   a) 6 9 4 12 5   b) 7 4 8 6 11 9   c) 42 39 36 41 41

   ☐ – ☐ = ☐   ☐ – ☐ = ☐   ☐ – ☐ = ☐

2. To find the **median** of a data set, put the data in order. Count from either end until you reach the middle.

   Example 1:   *Example 2:*

   2   3   ⑥   7   11   2   3   (7   9)   11   15

   The median   The median is half way
   is 6.   between 7 and 9.
                                      The median is 8.

   What number is half way between …

   a) 5 and 7?   b) 12 and 14?   c) 25 and 35?   d) 11 and 15?   e) 13 and 17?   f) 8 and 8?

   _____   _____   _____   _____   _____   _____

3. Circle the middle number or numbers. Find the median.

   a) 2 4 6 7 8   b) 2 3 3 8   c) 7 9 13 14 26   d) 3 4 6 10 11 17

   _____   _____   _____   _____

4. The data is in order. Circle the median then find the range of data below and above the median.
   Is the data spread out more above or below the median?

   a) 3 4 4 ④ 5 9 11   b) 13 17 20 25 26 27 30

   range *below* median: | 4 | – | 3 | = | 1 | range *below* median: ☐ – ☐ = ☐

   range *above* median: | 11 | – | 4 | = | 7 | range *above* median: ☐ – ☐ = ☐

   The data is spread out more __above__   The data is spread out more _____
   the median.   *above/below*   the median.   *above/below*

   c) 2 3 3 4 5 9 11 12 13   d) 430 435 440 450 460 480 510 540

   range *below* median: ☐ – ☐ = ☐   range *below* median: ☐ – ☐ = ☐

   range *above* median: ☐ – ☐ = ☐   range *above* median: ☐ – ☐ = ☐

   The data is spread out more _____   The data is spread out more _____
   the median.   *above/below*   the median.   *above/below*

1. Move one block so that all stacks have the same number of blocks.

   Example: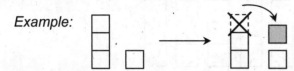

   a)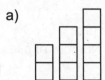

   b)

   c)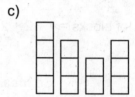

2. Move enough blocks so that all stacks have the same number of blocks.
   The **mean** is the number of blocks in each stack.

   a)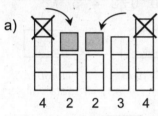

   4 2 2 3 4

   Mean: _____3_____

   b)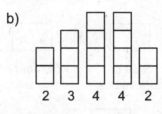

   2 3 4 4 2

   Mean: _____

   c)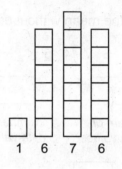

   1 6 7 6

   Mean: _____

3. Find the mean by drawing stacks and then moving blocks.

   a)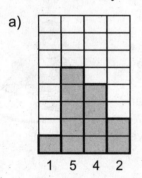

   1 5 4 2

   Mean: _____

   b)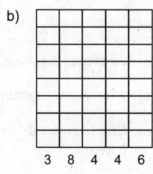

   3 8 4 4 6

   Mean: _____

   c)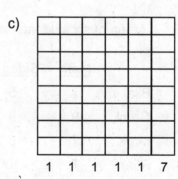

   1 1 1 1 1 7

   Mean: _____

   d)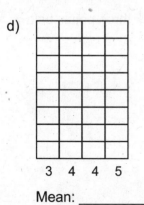

   3 4 4 5

   Mean: _____

   e)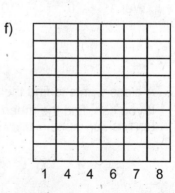

   2 3 3 4 8

   Mean: _____

   f)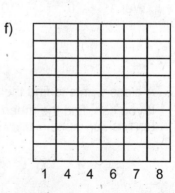

   1 4 4 6 7 8

   Mean: _____

4.

4   2   2   3   4

Number of blocks = 4 + 2 + 2 + 3 + 4 = 15

3   3   3   3   3

Mean = Number of blocks in each pile
= Total number of blocks ÷ Number of piles

So **mean = sum of data values ÷ number of data values**.

Find the mean without using blocks.

a) 1   3   7   4   5

☐ ÷ ☐

Sum of data values   *Number of data values*

= ☐

Mean

b) 1   8   5   10

☐ ÷ ☐

Sum of data values   *Number of data values*

= ☐

Mean

c) 0   0   2   4   5   7

☐ ÷ ☐

Sum of data values   *Number of data values*

= ☐

Mean

5. A group of six students wrote two tests (each out of 10).

	Math	Science
Bilal	7	5
Gorck	9	9
Mark	7	8
Ryan	7	10
Tasfia	6	6
Wei	6	10

a) What was the group's math mean?

b) What was the group's science mean?

c) On which test did they do better overall? Explain.

d) On which test did more students score at the mean?

e) On which test was the lowest mark three points below the mean?

6. A class wants to find the average of how many cousins they have.
   If you can, find the mean without using a calculator.
   HINT: Group the pairs that add to 10 or 20. (For example, 9 + 11 = 20.)

6   1   9   8   4   5   9   12   11   5

PDM4-15: Stem and Leaf Plots

The **leaf** of a number is its right-most digit.

The **stem** is all its digits <u>except</u> the right-most digit.
NOTE: The stem of a one-digit number is 0 since there are no digits except the right-most one.

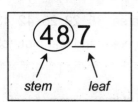

1. Underline the leaf. The first one is done for you.

   a) 12<u>3</u>   b) 31   c) 72   d) 4   e) 38

   f) 90   g) 801   h) 444   i) 322   j) 434

2. Circle the stem. The first two are done for you.

   a) 5   *no stem*   b) (3)7   c) 123   d) 31   e) 59

   f) 18   g) 6   h) 10   i) 4 321   j) 9 000

3. Now do both.

   a) 8   b) 83   c) 831   d) 8 310   e) 4 071

   f) 689   g) 907   h) 899   i) 3   j) 62 459

4. Write down a number with leaf 0: _____ and one with stem 0: _____ .

5. For each group of numbers, underline the numbers that have the same stem.

   a) 78 74 94   b) 89 90 91   c) 77 67 76   d) 371 379 391

   e) 263 26 265   f) 39 390 394   g) 5 782 578 574

   h) 34 341 3 340   i) 291 287 28 29

6. In each group of numbers, circle the stems and write the stems from smallest to largest.

   a) (1)3 9 8 (2)4 (6)4 (1)8 (2)5   _0_   _1_   _2_   _6_

   b) 26 29 48 53 27 9 44   ____ ____ ____ ____

   c) 102 98 86 76 103 95   ____ ____ ____ ____

   d) 99 134 136 128 104 97   ____ ____ ____ ____

   e) 942 998 965 1003 964   ____ ____ ____ ____

BONUS
7. Numbers with the same stem must have the same number of digits. True or False?

8. In the data set 38 29 26 42 43 34, the stems are 2, 3 and 4.

To build a stem and leaf plot, follow these steps.

Step 1:				Step 2:				Step 3:		
Write the stems in order, from smallest to largest.	stem	leaf		*Then write each leaf in the same row as its stem:*	stem	leaf		*Finally put the leaves in each row in order, from smallest to largest.*	stem	leaf
	2				2	96			2	69
	3				3	84			3	48
	4				4	23			4	23

For each plot, put the leaves in the correct order. Then list the data from smallest to largest.

a)

stem	leaf
2	1 4
3	8 6 5
5	3 2

→

stem	leaf
2	1 4
3	5 6 8
5	2 3

21   24   35   36   38   52   53

b)

stem	leaf
0	4
1	9 5
2	3 8 0

→

stem	leaf

___ ___ ___ ___ ___ ___

c)

stem	leaf
8	3 0
9	0 7 2
10	6

→

stem	leaf

___ ___ ___ ___ ___ ___

d)

stem	leaf
9	2 1 8
10	4 2 4
11	5 0

→

stem	leaf

___ ___ ___ ___ ___ ___

9. Use the following data to create stem and leaf plots. Part a) has been started for you.

a) 9 7 12 19 10

stem	leaf
0	9 7
1	

→

stem	leaf
0	7 9

rough work   *final answer*

b) 99 98 102 99 101

stem	leaf

→

stem	leaf

rough work   *final answer*

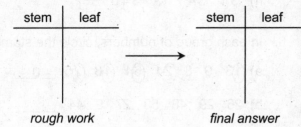

10. Anna and some friends ran a 5 km race. Their times were recorded:

26   32   38   29   40

a) What unit of measurement do you think they used? Seconds? Minutes? Hours? Days?

b) Make a stem and leaf plot of the data.

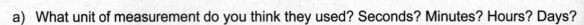

PDM4-15: Stem and Leaf Plots (continued)

11. Stem and leaf plots make it easy to find the smallest and largest data values.

   (i)   Look for the <u>smallest</u> leaf in the <u>first</u> row to find the **smallest** data value.

   (ii) Look for the <u>largest</u> leaf in the <u>last</u> row to find the **largest** data value.

   (iii) Then find the range.

a)

stem	leaf
8	247
9	89
10	014

Smallest: _82_

Largest: _104_

Range: ____

b)

stem	leaf
0	569
1	247
2	33

Smallest: ____

Largest: ____

Range: ____

c)

stem	leaf
9	569
10	188
12	0

Smallest: ____

Largest: ____

Range: ____

12. Find the data value that occurs twice in each stem and leaf plot.

a)

stem	leaf
8	569
10	188
12	0

____108____

b)

stem	leaf
0	3449
1	012
2	347

_____

c)

stem	leaf
0	89
1	147
2	266

_____

13. The **mode** of a data set is the number that occurs most often. Find the mode.

a)

stem	leaf
9	334
10	00016
11	225

Mode: _____

b)

stem	leaf
3	22227
4	333
5	48
6	099

Mode: _____

c)

stem	leaf
3	2278
4	56699
5	03336
6	799

Mode: _____

14. The class marks on a test were:

63	78	84	72	69	5̶8̶	74
87	91	73	75	5̶4̶	65	75
82	69	68	71	73	5̶9̶	74

a) Complete stem and leaf plot.

b) Circle the most common mark range:
   50–59   60–69   70–79   80–89   90–99

c) How does a stem and leaf plot make it easy to see the most common mark range? Explain.

Stem	Leaves of test marks								
5	4	8	9						

PDM4-16: Outcomes

The different ways an event can happen are called **outcomes** of the event.

When Alice plays a game of cards with a friend, there are three possible outcomes: Alice (1) wins, (2) loses or (3) the game ends without a winner or a loser (this is sometimes called a **tie** or a **draw**).

1. Fill in the chart.

		Possible Outcomes	Number of Outcomes
a)		You spin a 3 or a 4.	2
b)			
c)			
d)			
e)			
f)			

2. Draw a marble from a box. How many different outcomes are there in each of the following cases?

a)

b)

c)

d)

_____ outcomes   _____ outcomes   _____   _____

When an event is expected to occur exactly half the time, we say that there is an **even** chance of the event occurring.

- On the spinner shown, there is an even chance of spinning yellow.
- When you flip a coin, there is an even chance of flipping a head (and there is also an even chance of flipping a tail).

---

1. Shade <u>half</u> of the pie.

a)

____ pieces in half the pie

____ pieces in the pie

b)

____ pieces in half the pie

____ pieces in the pie

c)

____ pieces in half the pie

____ pieces in the pie

2. Divide by skip counting by 2s.

a) 10 ÷ 2 = ____   b) 12 ÷ 2 = ____   c) 18 ÷ 2 = ____   d) 20 ÷ 2 = ____   e) 16 ÷ 2 = ____

f) 8 ÷ 2 = ____   g) 4 ÷ 2 = ____   h) 14 ÷ 2 = ____   i) 6 ÷ 2 = ____   j) 22 ÷ 2 = ____

3. Fill in the chart.

Number	10	8	14	16	20
Half the Number	5				
Sum	<u>5</u> + <u>5</u> = 10	__ + __ = 8	__ + __ = 14	__ + __ = 16	__ + __ = 20

4. Draw circles to divide the lines into two equal sets.

a)

b)

c) | | | | | | | | |

5. There are 12 marbles in a box. Half are red. How many are red?

_____

6. A pie is cut in six equal pieces. How many pieces are half?

_____

7. Complete each statement by writing **more than half**, **half** or **less than half**.
   HINT: Start by finding half of the number by skip counting by 2s.

   a) 2 is _____less than half_____ of 6.   b) 3 is _____ of 8.

   c) 6 is _____ of 12.   d) 7 is _____ of 10.

   e) 11 is _____ of 14.   f) 5 is _____ of 10.

   g) 5 is _____ of 12.   h) 11 is _____ of 14.

   i) 7 is _____ of 8.   j) 6 is _____ of 10.

   k) 3 is _____ of 4.   l) 5 is _____ of 6.

8. First write the number of shaded pieces in the spinner, as well as the total number of pieces.
   Then circle the spinners where <u>half</u> the pieces are shaded.

   a) 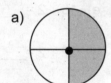   b)    c) 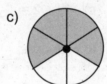   d) 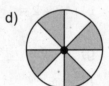   e)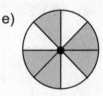

   ____ pieces   ____ pieces   ____ pieces   ____ pieces   ____ pieces
   shaded   shaded   shaded   shaded   shaded

   ____ pieces   ____ pieces   ____ pieces   ____ pieces   ____ pieces
   in total   in total   in total   in total   in total

9. Circle the spinners where there is an even chance of the spinner landing on a shaded region.
   Put a large 'X' through the pies where less than half the pieces are shaded.

PDM4-18: Even, Likely and Unlikely

The chances of an event can be described as …

- **"unlikely"** (the event is expected to happen <u>less</u> than half the time),
- **"likely"** (the event is expected to happen <u>more</u> than half the time), or
- **"even"** (exactly half the time).

---

1. Write **even** where you would expect to spin red <u>half</u> the time. Write **more than half** if you would expect to spin red more than half the time, and **less than half** otherwise.

a)

b)

c)

_____   _____   _____

d)

e)

f)

_____   _____   _____

2. Describe each event as **likely** or **unlikely**.

a)

b)

c)

d)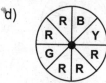

spinning red is: spinning blue is: spinning green is: spinning red is:

_____   _____   _____   _____

3. Describe the chances of each event as **unlikely**, **even** or **likely**.

a) 14 marbles in a box; 7 red marbles
   <u>Event</u>: You draw a red marble.

b) 14 marbles in a box; 5 red marbles
   <u>Event</u>: You draw a red marble.

_____   _____

c) 12 socks in a drawer; 8 black socks
   <u>Event</u>: You pull out a black sock.

d) 16 bills in a pocket; 9 $5 bills
   <u>Event</u>: You pull out a $5 bill.

_____   _____

4. Are your chances of rolling a number greater than 2 on a die **unlikely**, **even** or **likely**? Explain.

_____

_____

When two or more events have the same chance of occurring, the events are **equally likely**.

On spinner A, it is **equally likely** that you will spin red or green.

On spinner B, it is **equally likely** that you will spin red, green or yellow.

 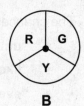

---

1.  Are your chances of spinning red and yellow equally likely? Explain your answer.

2.  Are your chances of spinning red and yellow equally likely? Explain your answer.

3. 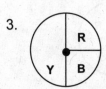 Are your chances of spinning red and yellow equally likely? Explain your answer.

4. Circle the spinners where spinning **red** and spinning **green** are equally likely.

a)   b)   c)   d)   e)

f)   g)   h)   i)   j)

5. For each spinner, which colour are you <u>most</u> likely to spin?

a)   b)

6. For each spinner, which colour are you <u>least</u> likely to spin?

a)   b)

_____   _____   _____   _____

7. For the spinner in Question 6 b), which two colours are you equally likely to spin? _____

   Explain. _____

- If an event cannot happen it is **impossible**. For example, rolling the number 8 on a die is **impossible** (because a die only has the numbers 1, 2, 3, 4, 5, and 6 on its faces).

- If an event <u>must</u> happen it is **certain**. For example, when you roll a die it is **certain** that you will roll a number less than 7.

Here, it is **likely** that you would spin yellow and **unlikely** that you would spin red:

1. Using the words **certain**, **likely**, **unlikely** or **impossible**, describe the likelihood of…

a)

spinning red

_____

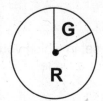
b)

spinning green

_____

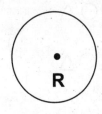
c)

spinning red

_____

d)

spinning yellow

_____

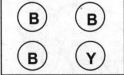
e)

picking blue

_____

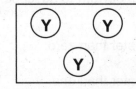
f)

picking yellow

_____

g)

picking green

_____

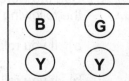
h)

picking red

_____

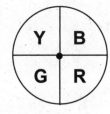
i)

spinning green

_____

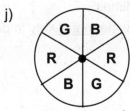
j)

spinning red

_____

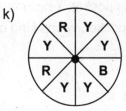
k)

spinning yellow

_____

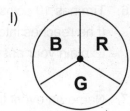
l)

spinning yellow

_____

2. Which colour of marble are you most likely to draw: red or blue? Explain your thinking.

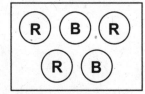

_____

_____

_____

3.

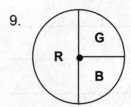

Complete the sentence:

If you choose a marble from the box ...

a) you are <u>most likely</u> to choose _____ .

b) you are <u>very unlikely</u> to choose _____ .

c) you <u>cannot possibly</u> choose _____ .

4. **A:**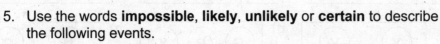

a) From which set of triangles and circles are you most likely to pick a triangle?

B: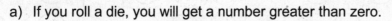

C: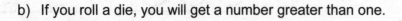

b) Circle the set in which you have an even chance of drawing a triangle or a circle.

D: △○△○○○△○

5. Use the words **impossible**, **likely**, **unlikely** or **certain** to describe the following events.

a) If you roll a die, you will get a number greater than zero.

b) If you roll a die, you will get a number greater than one.

c) You will see an elephant on the street today.

6. Tim has 10 coins in his pocket, 7 nickels and 3 dimes.
If he reaches into his pocket, which kind of coin is he <u>most likely</u> to pull out?
Explain your answer.

7. Name an event that is ...

a) impossible   b) likely   c) unlikely   d) certain

8. Draw a box of coloured balls where the probability of picking a red ball is ...

a) impossible   b) likely   c) unlikely   d) certain

9. Is each outcome on this spinner equally likely?
Explain.

A game of chance is **fair** if both players have the same chance of winning.

1. For each game, who has a better chance of winning: Player 1 or Player 2?
   If each player has the same chance of winning, write "The game is fair."

a)

Player 1 must spin red to win.

Player 2 must spin blue to win.

b)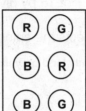

Player 1 must draw red to win.

Player 2 must draw blue to win.

c)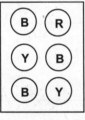

Player 1 must draw blue to win.

Player 2 must draw yellow to win.

d)

Player 1 must spin green to win.

Player 2 must spin yellow to win.

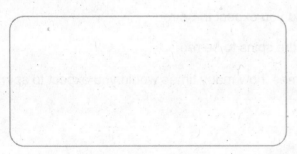

2. Gerome's favourite colour is blue and Iman's favourite colour is yellow. Design a spinner with <u>at least 4 regions</u> so that …

a) Iman is most likely to win.

b) both players have an <u>equal</u> chance of winning.

PDM4-22: Expectation

Kate plans to spin the spinner 15 times to see how many times it will land on yellow.

$\frac{1}{3}$ of the spinner is yellow so Kate **expects** to spin yellow $\frac{1}{3}$ of the time.

Kate finds $\frac{1}{3}$ of 15 by dividing by 3: $15 \div 3 = 5$

So she expects the spinner to land on yellow 5 times.

NOTE: The spinner may not actually land on yellow 5 times, but 5 is the <u>most likely</u> number of yellow spins.

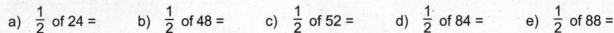

1. Using long division, find ...

   a) $\frac{1}{2}$ of 24 =   b) $\frac{1}{2}$ of 48 =   c) $\frac{1}{2}$ of 52 =   d) $\frac{1}{2}$ of 84 =   e) $\frac{1}{2}$ of 88 =

2. Sarah wants to divide her coin collection evenly into two boxes.
   How many coins should she put in each box if she has ...

   a) 6 coins?   b) 16 coins?   c) 26 coins?

   _____ coins in each box   _____ in each box   _____ in each box

   d) 22 coins?   e) 46 coins?   f) 50 coins?

   _____   _____   _____

3. 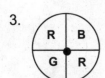 What fraction of your spins would you expect to be red?

   a) I would expect _____ of the spins to be red.

   b) If you spun the spinner 20 times, how many times would you expect to spin red?

   ┌───┐
   │   │
   └───┘

4. If you flip a coin repeatedly, what fraction of the throws would you expect to be heads? _____

5. If you flip a coin 12 times, how many times would you expect to flip heads? Explain your answer.

   ┌───┐
   │   │
   │   │
   │   │
   │   │
   │   │
   └───┘

6. How many times would you expect to flip heads if you flipped a coin?

   a) 40 times _____   b) 60 times _____

7. Find.

   a) $3\overline{)15}$ b) $3\overline{)18}$ c) $3\overline{)33}$ d) $3\overline{)51}$ e) $3\overline{)60}$

   f) $\frac{1}{3}$ of 9 is ____   g) $\frac{1}{3}$ of 18 is ____   h) $\frac{1}{3}$ of 39 is ____   i) $\frac{1}{3}$ of 75 is ____

   j) $\frac{1}{4}$ of 8 is ____   k) $\frac{1}{4}$ of 36 is ____   l) $\frac{1}{4}$ of 52 is ____   m) $\frac{1}{4}$ of 84 is ____

8. For each spinner below, what fraction of your spins would you expect to be red?

   a)   I would expect

   _____

   of the spins to be red.

   b)   I would expect

   _____

   of the spins to be red.

9. How many times would you expect to spin blue, if you spun the spinner ...

   a) 12 times?   b) 36 times?   c) 72 times?

   _____   _____   _____

10. How many times would you expect to spin yellow, if you spun the spinner...

   a) 16 times?   b) 48 times?   c) 92 times?

   _____   _____   _____

11. Sketch a spinner on which you would expect to spin red $\frac{3}{4}$ of the time.

12. On a spinner, the probability of spinning yellow is $\frac{2}{3}$.

    What is the probability of spinning a colour that is not yellow?
    Explain your answer with a picture.

Show your work for the problems on this page in your notebook.

1. If you flip a coin repeatedly, what <u>fraction</u> of the time would you expect to flip a head? A half? A third? A quarter?

   Explain your answer.

2. Flip a coin 10 times, making a tally of the number of heads and tails you got. Repeat the experiment five times.

   Did you always get approximately the same number of heads and tails each time?

3. Place the point of your pencil inside a paper clip in the middle of the circle. Hold the pencil still so you can spin the clip around the pencil.

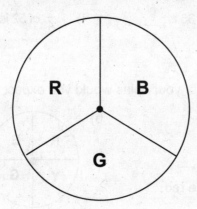

   a) If you spin the spinner 12 times, how many times would you predict spinning red? Show your work.

      HINT: Think of dividing 12 spins into 3 equal parts.

   b) Spin the spinner 12 times. Make a tally of your results. Did your results match your expectations? Explain.

4.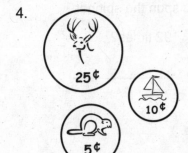

   You have 3 coins in your pocket: a nickel (5¢), a dime (10¢), and a quarter (25¢). You reach in and pull out a pair of coins.

   a) What are all the possible combinations of two coins you could pull out?

   b) How many outcomes are there?

   c) Would you expect to pull a pair of coins that add up to 30¢? Are the chances likely or unlikely?

   d) How did you solve the problem (Did you use a list? A picture? A calculation? Or a combination of these things?)

1. Join the dots in the given column OR row.

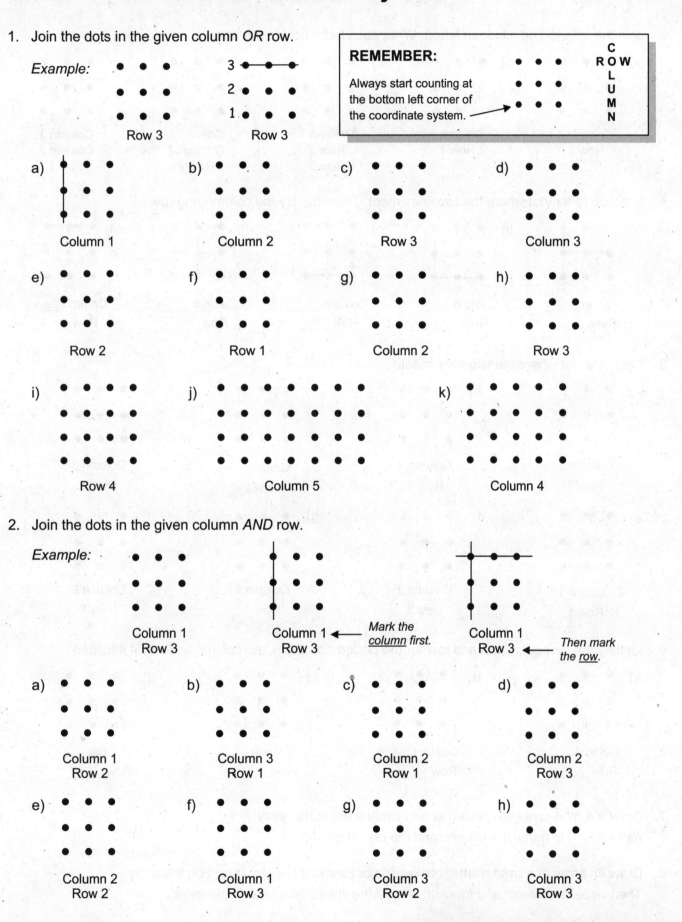

2. Join the dots in the given column AND row.

3. Join the dots to find a hidden letter! Write each letter beside the array.

a)
Column 2
Row 3

b)
Column 1
Row 1

c)
Column 1
Row 2
Row 3

d)
Column 1
Column 3
Row 2

e)
Column 1
Column 3
Row 1

4. First, circle the dot where the two lines meet. Then identify the column and row.

a)
Column _____
Row _____

b)
Column _____
Row _____

c)
Column _____
Row _____

d)
Column _____
Row _____

e)
Column _____
Row _____

5. Circle the dot where the two lines meet.

a)
Column 1
Row 3

b)
Column 2
Row 2

c)
Column 1
Row 2

d)
Column 3
Row 3

e)
Column 1
Row 1

f)
Column 2
Row 3

g)
Column 2
Row 1

h)
Column 3
Row 1

6. Identify the proper column and row for the circled dot. (Mark the column and row if it helps.)

a)
Column _____
Row _____

b)
Column _____
Row _____

c)
Column _____
Row _____

d)
Column _____
Row _____

7. Draw a 4-by-4 array on grid paper and circle a dot in the array.
   Ask a friend to name the column and the row of the dot.

8. Draw an array and write a letter backwards or forwards (i.e. ⊢ or ⊣) on the array.
   Then write the column and row numbers of the lines that make up the letter.

Josh slides a dot from one position to another. **Slides or translations** may be described using the words right, left, up and down.

Example: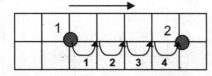

To move the dot from position 1 to position 2, Josh **slides** the dot **4 units right**.

1. How many units <u>right</u> did the dot slide from position 1 to position 2?

a)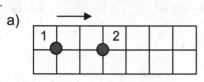

_____ units right

b)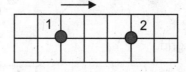

_____

c)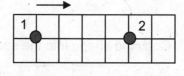

_____

2. How many units <u>left</u> did the dot slide from position 1 to position 2?

a)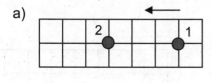

_____ units left

b)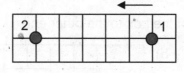

_____

c)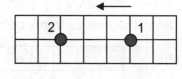

_____

3. Slide the dot …

a) 5 units right.

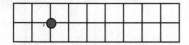

b) 4 units left.

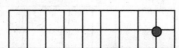

c) 7 units right.

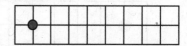

4. How many units <u>right</u> and how many units <u>down</u> did the dot slide from position 1 to position 2?

a)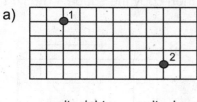

___ units right ___ units down

b)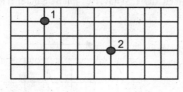

___ units right ___ units down

c)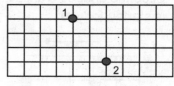

___ units right ___ units down

5. Slide the dot …

a) 3 units right; 3 units down.

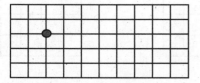

b) 5 units left; 2 units up.

c) 6 units left; 4 units down.

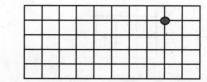

G4-22: Slides

1. Copy the shape into the second grid.
   HINT: Make sure your shape is in the same position relative to the dot.

   a) 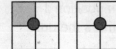 b)   c) 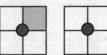 d)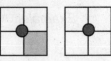

   e)   f) 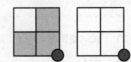 g) 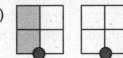 h)

2. Copy the shape into the second grid.

   a)   b)   c)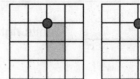

3. Slide the shapes from one end of the box to the other end.

   a) 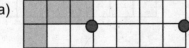 b) 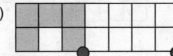 c)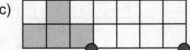

4. Slide the shapes 4 units left.

   a) 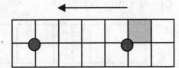 b) 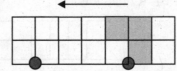 c)

5. Slide the shapes 3 units in the direction shown. First slide the dot, then copy the shape. The first one is started for you.

   a) 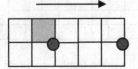 b) 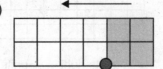 c)

6. Slide the dot three units down, then copy the shape.

   a)   b)   c)   d)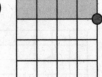

G4-23: Slides (Advanced)

In a **slide** (or translation), the figure moves in a straight line without turning. The image of a slide is congruent to the original figure.

Helen slides (or translates) a shape to a new position by following these steps:

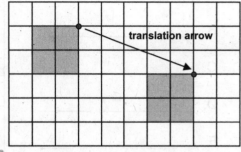

1. Draw a dot in a corner of the figure.
2. Slide the dot (in this case 5 right and 2 down).
3. Draw the image of the figure.

Join the two dots with a translation arrow to show the direction of the slide.

Slide the box 5 right and 2 down.

---

1. Slide each shape 4 boxes to the right. (Start by putting a dot on one of the corners of the figure. Slide the dot four boxes right, then draw the new figure.)

a)

b)
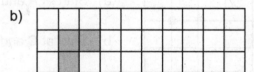

c)
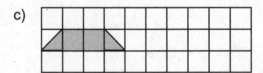

d)
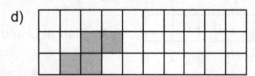

2. Slide each figure 5 boxes to the right and 2 boxes down.

a)
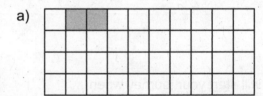

b)
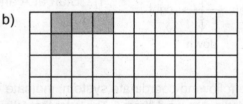

3. Slide the shapes in the grids below. Then describe the slide by writing how many boxes you moved the figure horizontally (right or left) and how many boxes you moved it vertically (up or down).

a)
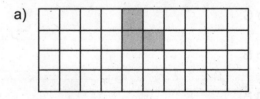

My slide: _____

b)
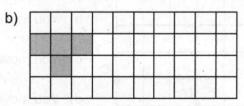

My slide: _____

BONUS

4.
A			B	

Marco says shape B is a slide of shape A. Is he correct? Explain.

G4-24: Grids and Maps

1. How many units (right/left and up/down) must the star slide to reach the following points?

A. _____right 3, up 1_____

B. _____

C. _____

D. _____

E. _____

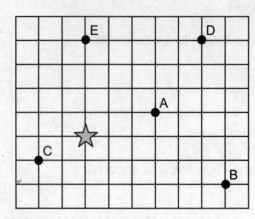

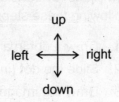

2. Using the following coordinate system, describe your path.

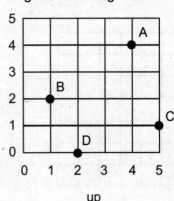

a) Start at A and go to B: | 3 left, 2 down

b) Start at C and go to D:

c) Start at B and go to C:

d) Start at D and go to B:

e) Start at A and go to C:

f) Start at A and go to D:

3. Using the following coordinate system, indicate where you will <u>start</u> your journey when …
   HINT: Underline the word "from." The letter that follows the word "from" is where you start.

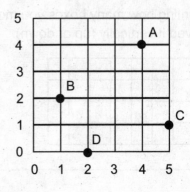

a) You move <u>from</u> A to B: | start at A

b) You move to B from C:

c) You move from D to B:

d) You move to D from A:

e) You move to C from A:

f) You move from A to C:

Geometry 2

4. Answer the following questions using the coordinate system.
    HINT: Underline the word "from" in each question.

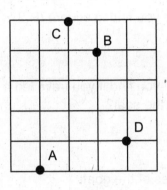

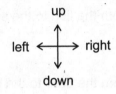

a) What point is 3 units right and 1 up from A? ⬜

b) What point is 2 units left and 4 up from D? ⬜

c) What point is 1 unit down and 1 right of C? ⬜

d) Describe how to get from point B to point D:

e) Describe how to go to point B from point A:

f) Describe how to get to point A from point C:

5. Answer the following questions using the coordinate system.

a) What building is 4 blocks west and 2 blocks north of the house?

b) What building is 2 blocks east and 1 block south of the school?

c) What is 2 blocks south and 1 block east of the school?

d) Describe how to get from the park to the gym:

e) Describe how to go to the pool from the house:

f) Describe how to go to the park from the school:

6. The grid shows the location of some animal cages at a zoo.
   NOTE: Each edge on the grid represents 10 m.

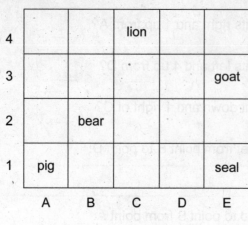

a) What animal would you find in square (B,2)?

b) What animal would you find if you travelled 4 grid squares west from the seal?

c) Give the coordinates of the goat:

d) Describe how to get from the lion to the seal:

e) Describe how to get from the bear to the goat:

7. Use the following clues to figure out where all the children sit.

   ✎ Walk 2 desks up and 1 desk right from Erin to find John's seat.

   ✎ Tom is 1 desk up from Abdul.

   ✎ Jane is between Erin and Abdul.

   ✎ Walk 1 desk right and 1 desk up from George to find Mary's desk.

   ✎ Ed is 1 desk left of George.

   ✎ Walk 2 desks left and 2 desks up from Abdul to find Clara's desk.

	George	
Erin		Abdul

8. Describe the path Jacob took to sail from his starting point (A) to his finishing point (F).

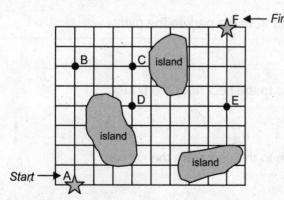

a) From A (start) to B: _____

b) From B to C: _____

c) From C to D: _____

d) From D to E: _____

e) From E to F (finish): _____

1. Use the given map of Canada to answer the following questions.

Each coordinate location should be written as (column, row), for example: **(A,3)**.

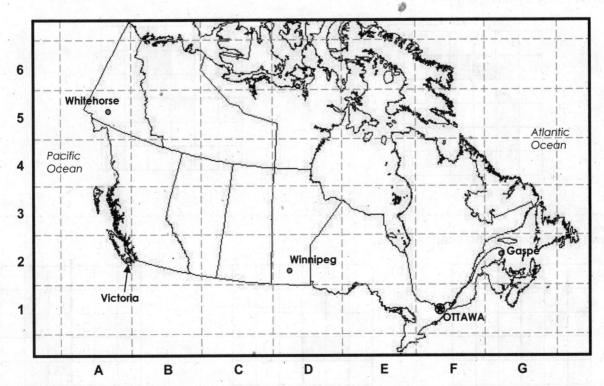

a) What are the coordinates of Ottawa (the capital city of Canada)?

b) What are the coordinates of Whitehorse, Yukon Territory?

c) What are the coordinates of Winnipeg, Manitoba?

d) What are the coordinates of Gaspé, Quebec?

e) **(A,2)** are the coordinates of which city?

f) **(G,5)** is in which body of water?

g) **(F,2)** is in which province?

2. **Secret Squares**

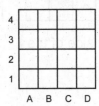

In this game, Player 1 draws a 4 x 4 grid as shown and picks a square.

Player 2 tries to guess the square by giving its coordinates.

Each time Player 2 guesses, Player 1 writes the distance (counted horizontally and vertically) between the guessed square and the hidden square.

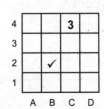

For instance, if Player 1 has chosen square B2 (✓) and Player 2 guesses C4, Player 1 writes 3 in the guessed square. (Distances on the grid are counted horizontally and vertically, <u>never</u> diagonally.)

The game ends when Player 2 guesses the correct square.

Alan **reflects** the shape by flipping it over the mirror line. Each point on the figure flips to the opposite side of the mirror line, but stays the same distance from the line. Alan checks to see that his reflection is drawn correctly by using a mirror.

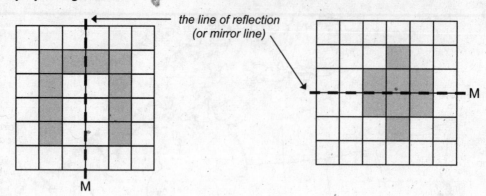

the line of reflection
(or mirror line)

1. Draw the reflection of the shapes below.

a)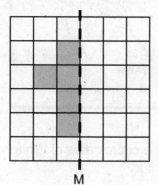

b)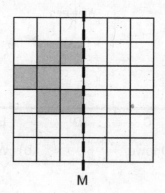

c)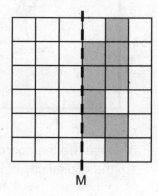

2. Draw the reflection, or flip, of the shapes.

a)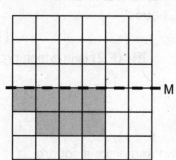

b)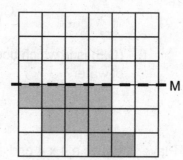

c)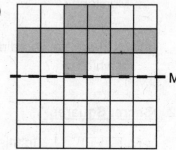

3. Draw your own shape in the box below. Now draw the flip of the shape on the other side of the mirror line.

BONUS
Are the shapes on either side of the mirror line congruent? Explain your answer.

G4-27: Reflections (Advanced)

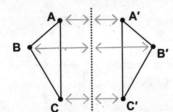

When a point is reflected in a mirror line, the point and the image of the point are the same distance from the mirror line.

A figure and its image are congruent but face in opposite directions.

---

1. Reflect the point P through the mirror line M.

a) 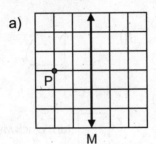 b) 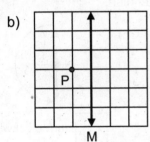 c) 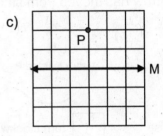 d)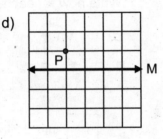

2. Reflect the set of points P, Q, R through the mirror line.

a) 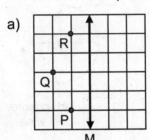 b) 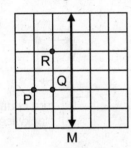 c) 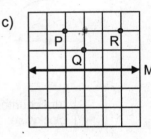 d)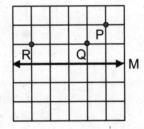

3. Reflect the figure by first reflecting the points on the figure.

a) 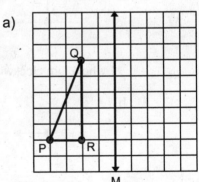 b) 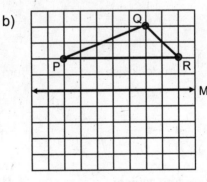 c)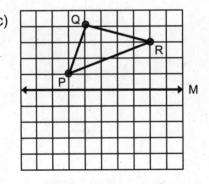

4. Sketch what each letter would look like reflected in the mirror line.
   REMEMBER: The reflection must face in the opposite direction to the figure.

a)   b)   c)   d)   e)

Geometry 2

G4-28: Rotations

Alice wants to **rotate** this arrow
$\frac{1}{4}$ of a turn clockwise:

Step 1:
*She draws a
circular arrow to
show how far the
arrow should turn.*

Step 2:
*She draws
the final position
of the arrow.*

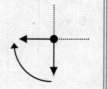

1. Write how far each arrow has moved from start to finish.

a)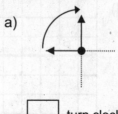

▢ turn clockwise

b)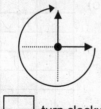

▢ turn clockwise

c)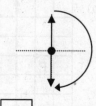

▢ turn clockwise

d)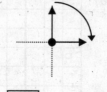

▢ turn clockwise

2. Write how far each arrow has moved counter clockwise from start to finish.

a)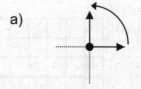

▢ turn counter
clockwise

b)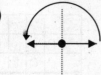

▢ turn counter
clockwise

c)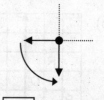

▢ turn counter
clockwise

d)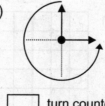

▢ turn counter
clockwise

3. Using Alice's method, show where the arrow would be after each turn.

a)

$\frac{1}{4}$ turn clockwise

b)

$\frac{3}{4}$ turn clockwise

c)

$\frac{1}{2}$ turn clockwise

d)

1 whole turn clockwise

e)

$\frac{1}{2}$ turn counter
clockwise

f)

$\frac{1}{4}$ turn counter
clockwise

g)

1 whole turn
counter clockwise

h)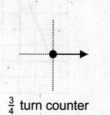

$\frac{3}{4}$ turn counter
clockwise

i)

$\frac{1}{4}$ turn counter
clockwise

j)

$\frac{3}{4}$ turn clockwise

k)

$\frac{1}{2}$ turn counter
clockwise

l)

$\frac{1}{2}$ turn clockwise

G4-29: Rotations (Advanced)

1. Show what the figure would look like after the rotation. First rotate the dark line, then draw the rest of the figure.

a)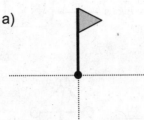

$\frac{1}{4}$ turn clockwise

b)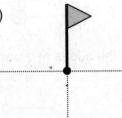

$\frac{1}{2}$ turn clockwise

c)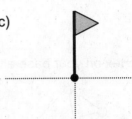

$\frac{3}{4}$ turn clockwise

d)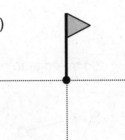

1 whole turn clockwise

e)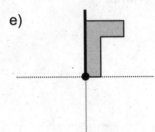

$\frac{1}{4}$ turn clockwise

f)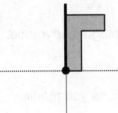

$\frac{1}{2}$ turn clockwise

g)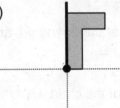

$\frac{3}{4}$ turn counter clockwise

h)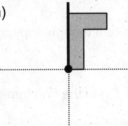

1 whole turn clockwise

i)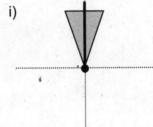

$\frac{1}{4}$ turn clockwise

j)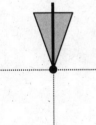

$\frac{3}{4}$ turn clockwise

k)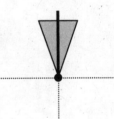

$\frac{1}{4}$ turn counter clockwise

l)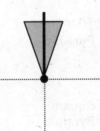

$\frac{1}{2}$ turn clockwise

m)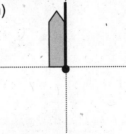

$\frac{1}{4}$ turn clockwise

n)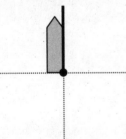

$\frac{3}{4}$ turn clockwise

o)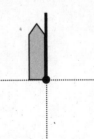

$\frac{1}{4}$ turn counter clockwise

p)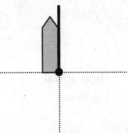

$\frac{1}{2}$ turn clockwise

BONUS
2. Draw a figure on grid paper. Draw a dot on one of its corners.
   Show what the figure would look like if you rotated it a quarter turn clockwise around the dot.

jump math
MULTIPLYING POTENTIAL.

Geometry 2

G4-30: Building Pyramids

To make a **skeleton** for a **pyramid**, start by making a base.
Your base might be a triangle or a square.

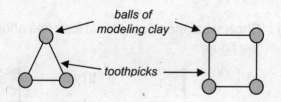

Now add an edge to each vertex on your base and join the edges at a point.

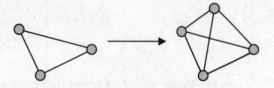

Triangular Pyramid

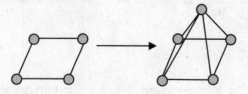

Square Pyramid

Make a triangular pyramid, a square pyramid, and a pentagonal pyramid.

----

1. Fill in the first three rows of the chart. Use the skeletons you made.

	Draw Shape of Base	Number of Sides of Base	Number of Edges of Pyramid	Number of Vertices of Pyramid
Triangular Pyramid				
Square Pyramid				
Pentagonal Pyramid				
Hexagonal Pyramid				

2. Describe the pattern in each column of your chart.

3. Use the pattern to fill in the row for the hexagonal pyramid.

4. What relationship do you see between the number of sides in the <u>base</u> of a pyramid and the number of edges in the pyramid?

Geometry 2

G4-31: Building Prisms

To make a skeleton for a **prism**, start by making a base (as you did for a pyramid). However, your prism will also need a top, so you should make a copy of the base.

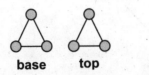

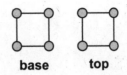

Now join each vertex in the base to a vertex in the top.

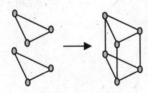

----

1. Fill the first three rows of the chart, using the skeletons you made.

	Draw Shape of Base	Number of Sides of Base	Number of Edges of Prism	Number of Vertices of Prism
Triangular Prism				
Rectangular Prism				
Pentagonal Prism				
Hexagonal Prism				

2. Describe the pattern in each column of your chart.

3. Use the pattern to fill in the row for the hexagonal prism.

4. What relationship do you see between the number of sides in the <u>base</u> of a prism and the number of edges in the prism?

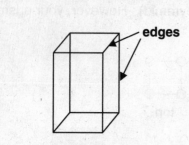

edges

Candice builds a **skeleton** of a
rectangular prism using wire.

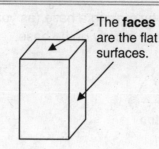

The **faces**
are the flat
surfaces.

She covers the skeleton
with paper.

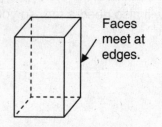

Faces
meet at
edges.

The dotted lines show the
<u>hidden</u> edges.

1. Draw dotted lines to show the hidden edges.

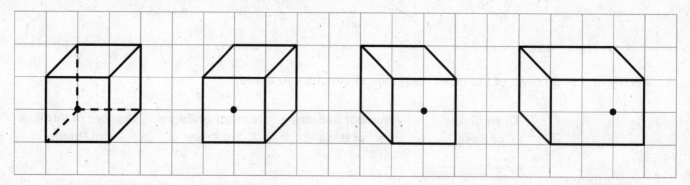

2. Shade all of the edges (the first one is started for you).
   Count the edges as you shade them.

a)

____ edges

b)

____ edges

c)

____ edges

d)

____ edges

e)

____ edges

f)

____ edges

g)

____ edges

h)

____ edges

3. Vertices are the points where the edges of a shape meet.
   Put a dot on each vertex (the first one is started for you). Count the vertices.

a)

____ vertices

b)

____ vertices

c)

____ vertices

d)

____ vertices

4. Shade the …

front face:

a)   b)   c)   d)

back face:

e)   f)   g)   h)

side faces:

i)   j)   k)   l)

top and **bottom** faces:

m)   n)   o)   p)

back face:

q)   r)   s)   t)

bottom face:

u)   v)   w)   x)

5. Shade the edges that would be hidden if the skeleton was covered in paper and placed on a table.

a)   b)   c)   d)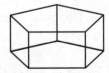

BONUS

6. Shade the edges that would be hidden if the skeleton was covered with paper and was hung above you in the position shown.

G4-33: Prisms and Pyramids

The solid shapes in the figure are called **3-D shapes**.

Faces are the flat surfaces of a shape, **edges** are where two faces meet, and **vertices** are the points where 3 or more faces meet.

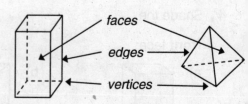

Pyramids have a **point** opposite the base. The base of the shape is a polygon; for instance, a triangle, a quadrilateral or a square (like the pyramids in Egypt), a pentagon, etc.

Prisms do not have a point. Their faces are the same at both ends of the shape.

----

1. Count the faces of each shape.

a)

_____ faces

b)

_____ faces

c)

_____ faces

d)

_____ faces

e)

_____ faces

f)

_____ faces

g)

_____ faces

h)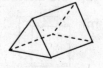

_____ faces

2. Using a set of 3-D shapes and the chart below as reference, answer the following questions.

A	B	C	D	E
Square Pyramid	**Triangular Pyramid**	**Rectangular Prism**	**Cube**	**Triangular Prism**

a) Describe each shape in terms of its faces, vertices and edges. The first one has been done.

	A	B	C	D	E
Number of Faces	5				
Number of Vertices	5				
Number of Edges	8				

b) Did any shapes have the same number of faces / vertices / edges? If so, which shapes share which properties?

Geometry 2

G4-34: Prism and Pyramid Bases

Melissa is exploring differences between pyramids and prisms. She discovers that ...

- • **A pyramid** has **one base**.
  (There is one exception – in a triangular
  pyramid, any face is a base.)

Example:

- • **A prism** has **two bases**.
  (There is one exception – in a
  rectangular prism any pair of opposite
  faces are bases.)

Example: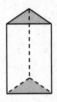

IMPORTANT NOTE:
The base(s) are not always on the "bottom" or "top" of the shape.

- -

TEACHER:
The activity that goes with this worksheet will help your students identify the base of a 3-D figure.

1. Shade a base <u>and</u> circle the point of the following pyramids. The first one is done for you.
   NOTE: The base will not necessarily be on the "bottom" of the shape (but it is *always* at the end opposite the point).

a)   b)   c)   d)

e)   f)   g)   h)

2. Shade a pair of bases for each prism.
   REMEMBER: Unless all its faces are rectangles, a <u>prism</u> has <u>two bases</u>.

a)   b)   c) 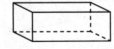 d)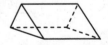

e)  f)   g)   h)

Geometry 2

3. Shade the bases of the following figures.

    Be careful! Some will have two bases (the prisms) and others will have only one (the pyramids).

a) 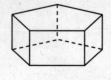   b)   c) 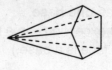   d)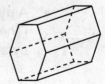

e)   f) 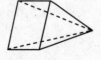   g) 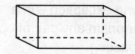   h)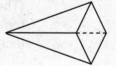

i)   j) 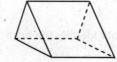   k)   l)

m)    n)   o)   p)

BONUS

4. Melissa has many prisms and pyramids. Circle the ones that have **all congruent faces**.

a)   b) 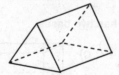   c)   d)

e)   f)   g) 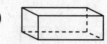   h)

1. Circle all the **pyramids**.
   Put an "X" through all the **prisms**.

2. Match each shape to its name. The first one has been done for you.

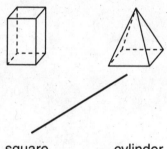   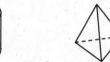

| square pyramid | cylinder | triangular prism | cone | rectangular prism | triangular pyramid |

3. a) Compare the shapes below. Use the chart to find properties that are the <u>same</u> and <u>different</u>.

Property	Rectangular Prism	Square Pyramid	Same?	Different?
Number of faces	6	5		✓
Shape of base				
Number of bases				
Number of faces that are <u>not</u> bases				
Shape of faces that are <u>not</u> bases				
Number of edges				
Number of vertices				

 b) Complete the following sentences:

"A rectangular prism and a square pyramid are the <u>same</u> in these ways ..."

"A rectangular prism and a square pyramid are <u>different</u> in these ways ..."

4. a) Complete the chart. Use actual 3-D shapes to help you.

   Colour the number of sides in each base to help you name the shape.

Shape	Picture of Base	Number of ...			Name
		edges	vertices	faces	

b) Circle the prisms.

c) Compare the number of vertices in each prism to the number of sides in the base.
   What do you notice?

  5. Write a paragraph outlining how the shapes are the <u>same</u> and how they are <u>different</u>.

a)

b)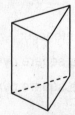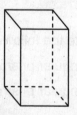

G4-35: Properties of Pyramids and Prisms (continued)

6. Sketch all the faces that make up the following 3-D shapes. The first one has been done for you.

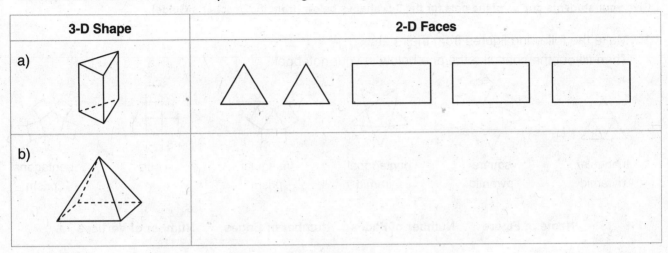

3-D Shape	2-D Faces
a)	
b)	

Show your work for parts c), d), and e) in your notebook.

c)   d)   e)

7. Match the description of the figure with its name.

_____ cone

_____ triangular prism

_____ cube

_____ cylinder

_____ triangular pyramid

A. I have 6 congruent faces.

B. I have 5 faces: 2 triangles and 3 rectangles.

C. I have 4 faces. Each face is a triangle.

D. I have 2 circular bases and a curved face.

E. I have 1 circular base and a curved face.

8. "I have a square base." Name two 3-D solids that this sentence could describe.

9. Name the object you could make if you assembled the shapes.

a) 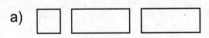   b)   c)

10. Sketch two faces that you can't see.

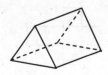

11.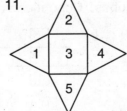

a) Which face of the net has the most vertices?

b) Which face shares a side with every other face?

12. Sketch a net for …

a) a triangular pyramid.   b) a rectangular pyramid.   c) a triangular prism.

Geometry 2

TEACHER:
Give your students copies of the nets for the 3-D shapes below (from the Teacher's Guide).

1. Make the following figures from their nets.
   Then fill out the chart like the one below in your notebook.

| triangular pyramid | square pyramid | pentagonal pyramid | triangular prism | cube | pentagonal prism |

Name of Figure	Number of Faces	Number of Edges	Number of Vertices

2. Draw the missing face for each net.

(i)   (ii)   (iii)

a) What is the shape of each missing face? _____

b) Are the nets pyramids or prisms? How do you know?

_____

3. Draw the missing face for each net.

(i) 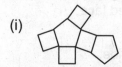   (ii)    (iii)

a) What is the shape of each missing face? _____

b) Are the nets pyramids or prisms? How do you know?

_____

4. Copy the following nets onto centimetre grid paper (use 4 grid squares for each face)
   Predict which nets will make cubes. Cut out each net and fold it to check your predictions.

a) 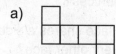   b) 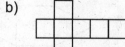   c)

d) 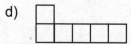   e)    f)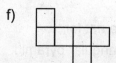

Eve sorts the following figures using a Venn diagram. She first decides on two properties that a figure might have. She then makes a chart.

A   **B**   **C**   **D**   **E**

Property	Figures with this property
1. One or more rectangular faces	
2. Fewer than 7 vertices	

1. a) Which figure(s) share both properties? _____

   b) Using the information in the chart above, complete the following Venn diagram.

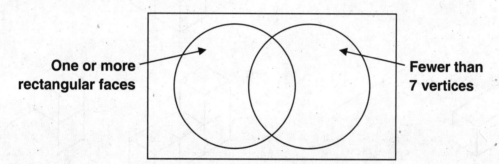

One or more rectangular faces   **Fewer than 7 vertices**

2. Complete both the chart and the Venn diagram below using the shapes A to E.

   a)

Property	Figures with this property
1. Triangular base	
2. Prism	

   b) Which figures share both properties? _____

   c) Using the information in the chart above, complete the following Venn diagram.

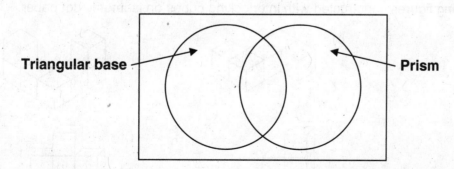

Triangular base   **Prism**

G4-38: Isoparametric Drawings

Follow these steps to draw a **cube** on isometric dots.

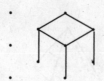

Step 1:
Draw a square with 4 vertices at 4 different dots.

Step 2:
Draw vertical lines at 3 vertices to touch the dots below.

Step 3:
Join the vertices.

---

1. Draw the following figures constructed with the interlocking cubes on isometric dot paper.

a)

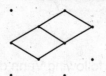

b)
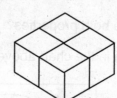
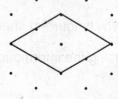

c)
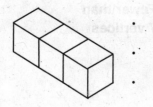

d)
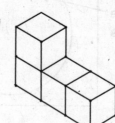
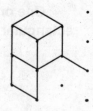

e)
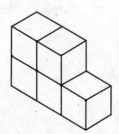
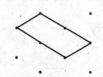

f)
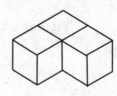

BONUS

2. Draw the following figures constructed with interlocking cubes on isometric dot paper.

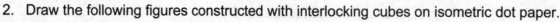

a)

b)

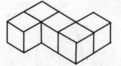

c)
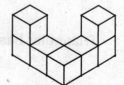

d)

e)

f)

G4-39: Isometric Drawings

1. Build the figures with blocks or interlocking cubes.

   a)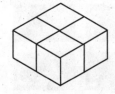

   b)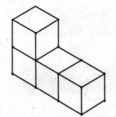

   c)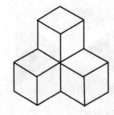

   c)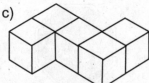

   e)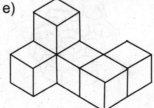

   f)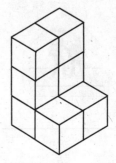

2. The numbers tell you how many blocks are stacked in each position.
   Fill in the missing numbers.

   a)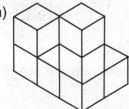
   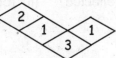

   b)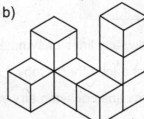
   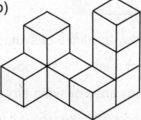

   c)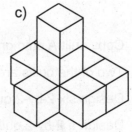

   d)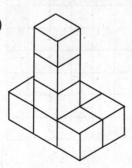

   e)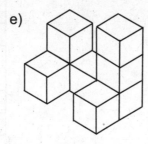

   f)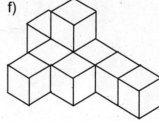

BONUS

3. Draw figures 2 a) and 2 b) on isometric dot paper.

jump math
MULTIPLYING POTENTIAL

Geometry 2

1. Draw any lines of symmetry you see in the flags.

    a)

    b)

    c)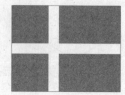

2. What polygons are suggested by the pictures?

    a)

    b)

    c)

    _____   _____   _____

3. Quilts are often made by sewing together half coloured squares.

    A    B   C

    a) Copy quilt A onto grid paper. Draw any lines of symmetry that you see.

    b) Two of the quilts are reflections of each other. Copy them on grid paper. Draw a line of reflection.

    c) Design six 2-by-2 quilts. Draw any lines of symmetry you see.

    d) Design a 2-by-2 quilt and show how it would look if it were ... (i) reflected   (ii) rotated 90°

4. Describe how to get to the centre of the garden maze.

    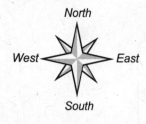

    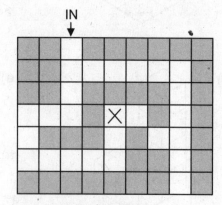

5. a) What kind of pyramid is the Egyptian pyramid?

    b) Look for prisms, cones and cylinders in magazine pictures.

    c) Find any objects in the classroom that have parts that are prisms, pyramids, cones, and cylinders.

       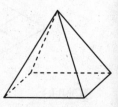